Hello Beautiful

SEE YOURSELF

Through the Father's Eyes

Eve M. Harrell

Dedicated to Sandy Knap
Thank you for teaching us to always seek Jesus.
May we always remember and never forget.

Thank you to Meagan Idol for teaching me that
"I am fearfully and wonderfully made."

Thank you to all my girls,
you inspire me to see myself through The Father's Eyes.

Special Thank You to my Beautiful contributors!
I am honored to share the encouragement that you show in your
everyday life. Keep shining the light of Jesus ladies! He will do great
things in and through your hearts.

This book is great for preteens and teens alike; as an educator and a student, I have seen the need for a book like this. Each chapter is no more than a page or three and written in a letter format. Each chapter can be read not in sequential order as well. I love that there are places for notes - allowing the reader to mark up the book.

Jenna

I love this book! I felt like the author was talking directly to me. Each time I picked it up, I was pointed to how the Father views me: beautiful. Although designed for teens, I think all women can benefit from reading.

Beckie

I'm a mom to a houseful of daughters. I received a copy of Hello Beautiful: See Yourself through the Father's Eyes from the author. I enjoyed it so much that I bought a second copy for my tween. It's a great study to enjoy together. I'm thankful for this helpful tool as I guide my girls into wisdom and maturity in Christ. It's one of my greatest desires as a mom that they learn to see themselves the way the Father sees them. I believe Hello Beautiful will help moms and daughters alike to discover important truths about our identity in Christ.

Heather

This book is fantastic! It is so easy to read. I recommend this book for girls 12yrs - 30yrs old! It is geared toward teens, but the truth is good for every woman as well. I am 54 and I got a lot out of it!! Great truth and scripture references. I read this book on the beach. It was so good; I gave it to a 15 year old that was sitting beside me!

Karen

This book is beautifully written. I've laughed, cried, and just been so blessed by the gift it is to us women. Eve is a very gifted author who has such a beautiful way of telling the truth of God's love for us. Her words help open your eyes to see just how beautiful and unique you are.

Team Jireh

Hello Beautiful has been a tremendous blessing, not only to my family but also to all the young ladies we've been able to reach and touch with the words inside this inspirational! Great read for any age to truly find your beauty that lies within and to view yourselves through the Father's eyes.

Young Women of Change

TABLE OF CONTENTS

INTRODUCTION

An Open Letter to Girls Everywhere:

You inspire me. The spirit and energy you bring to this generation encourages me for the future. You pour hope into a weary culture through the desire you have for a better tomorrow. This hope, combined with your creativity, will help lead us there.

In 1983, there was a young girl lost in the pursuit of her identity. Through the grace of her Heavenly Father, she realized her value and purpose. He showed her the beauty she had within as He transformed her into the likeness of Christ. All while providing friends who taught her to laugh and let go. A gentle stirring in her spirit and encouragement from a caring mentor spawned a yearning to encourage the next generation with the hope she had found.

Admittedly, the decision to work with high school girls overwhelmed me. Did I want to go back to that insecure place? The answer turned into a resounding YES as I realized the great opportunity before me to encourage others. To be honest, I've found that not much has changed since 1983. Sure, the clothes, hairstyles and trends may be different, but the underlying emotions, insecurities, worries, and fears are still there.

Through the eyes of some amazing young women, I have watched the hand of God move. I am honored to see hearts changed, depression lifted, courage found and unconditional love realized as grace stirs them to action.

In response, I hope to share with you what God has taught me, through letters. I am collaborating with some of my young friends to share with you important and relevant truth. We all need encouragement, whether we are 13, 30 or 60. We all need to know the truth that WE ARE LOVED!

YOU need to know you are loved and God has a special plan just for you.

My prayer is that you will receive these truths and see yourself through the eyes of the One who loved you so much that He wrote your name in the palm of His hand.

Love Always,

Eve

Chapter 1
You Are Loved

*For as high as the heavens are above the earth, so great is his love
for those who fear him.*
Psalm 103:11

Hello Beautiful,

Once upon a time, a girl sat alone in her room. Every day

she asked the same questions as she looked in the mirror-

wondering who was out there to hear her heart.

Who loves me?

Why am I all alone?

Why can't I do anything right?

Are you too looking in the same mirror? Today dear one, I

am here to tell you that someone has heard your heart, *and you are*

not alone.

As I write to you, I am over 30,000 feet in the air, flying to a

1

business conference. Looking out of my window, I consider the sadness in the words of this prayer. I consider your own prayer today. Oh, if only I could share with you the beauty of the clouds below and the patchwork quilt of trees, land, and houses. Beautiful, there is so much beauty in our surroundings, a beauty that brings joy to heal our lonely hearts.

Did you know that when you look up at the sky, there is a new palette awaiting you? A beautiful palette, always pointing to the Creator who gives life, the One who loves you immensely. Yes, *you*, dear one.

Why am I writing to you? God has given me this moment in time to share a message. He wants you to know who He is and who you are. He sees you. He loves you and has heard your prayer. He wants you to know He has captured all your tears in the palm of his hand. Why now? Well, there is a saying, *Hindsight is 20/20.* Hindsight (or remembering the past with eyes wide open) is facing me in the mirror of my heart in an attempt to encourage and give hope. And not just to you dear one. But to so many, who like you, wonder if they are alone.

⇨**Reflection Time:** What is love? Is it just a four letter word? Or perhaps- is it far greater than we can ever imagine? Will you do me a favor, please? Take this very moment and write down what you think love is. Write the name of every person who has shown you love.

After you perform this exercise, place it where you'll see it. And over time, I would like you to update it as your understanding changes. I believe God has chosen this moment to take us on a journey to learn the beauty of love and the Heart of a Father. I believe He will change our hearts through His message of Love. **I challenge you to walk this journey with me. Let's do this, shall we?**⇦

***

I would like to introduce you to David. A king who wrote a beautiful book of worship called Psalms, David wrote for the One who created him. He penned words like these: *"You have searched me, Lord, and you know me. You know when I sit and when I rise; you perceive my thoughts from afar" (Psalm 139:1).* David wrote this book to God, our Creator and Heavenly Father. He wrote it in acknowledgment of the perfection God had created. While it is **about** God and **to** God, I believe He also wanted to share it with us as a reminder that we are not an accident. I believe that David wanted you to know that God knows you, loves you, values you, and has a unique plan just for you. Yes, the all-knowing, all-powerful God who is present everywhere knows **YOU**. He knows your every thought and holds your every tear. He knows when your belly is in knots, and He knows every fear. And most of all, He loves you with all of His being through every moment of your life.

Once a gawky 12-year old, I was so in need of acceptance from others. Negative emotions had taken control of my mind. Can you relate? You feel disappointment when it appears nobody wants to hang out, or discouragement when you peer into the mirror and think, *"How could anyone like a girl like me?"* Yes, I have been there.

4

I remember the feelings of anxiety when I faced the bully on the bus. I cannot forget the heartbreak over the boy who wouldn't give me the time of day. In the moment, it's easy to get lost in the emotion of it all, forgetting that there is Someone who is present and loves us very much. So I encourage you to listen to David, *"a man after God's own heart."* He knew the truth we are seeking.

Read an excerpt from David's heart:

*"For you created my inmost being; you knit me together in my mother's womb. I praise you because **I am fearfully and wonderfully made**; your works are wonderful, I know that full well. My frame was not hidden from you when I was made in the secret place, when I was woven together in the depths of the earth. Your eyes saw my unformed body; all the days ordained for me were written in your book before one of them came to be. How precious to me are your thoughts God! How vast is the sum of them! Were I to count them, they would outnumber the grains of sand- when I awake, I am still with you"* (*Psalm 139:13-18*).

Oh how I wish someone had shared with me the depths of

the meaning in this letter. But here I am, sharing with you and all who need to read and write this truth on their hearts.

You are loved.

El Shaddai, Almighty God, created you in his image. **YES, YOU!** This scripture says He created your inmost being; He knit you together in your mother's womb. Soak that in for a moment.

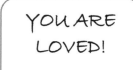

Your heavenly Father knew every part of you even before your mom and dad met you- every freckle, every pimple, every mole, and every hair on your head. Not only does He know you, He thinks of you, even today! This scripture, written by David, allows us to peer into the heart of our Creator to see His love for His creation. YOU!

I have so much I want to share with you. So much I need to say. Many letters will follow. I hope they will encourage and remind you just how precious you are.

Hear my heart, Beautiful. Your Father hears how sad you are. He knows how much you want others to like you. He wants you to know He loves you. He has placed and will continue to place others in your life who love you just as you are. Yes, gawkiness, freckles, pimples and all! The Creator of the universe, the One who placed every star in the sky and painted this perfect palette, says in His Word that *you are special*, and He meets you right where you are with a message:

He is here and He loves you!

***

Today I have a **call to action** for you. Ready?

Find a journal. It doesn't have to be fancy; it can be a simple notebook, something you can use as you read the letters to follow. (You can also use the empty space at the end of every letter). Today I would like you to begin by writing yourself a letter. Be as creative as you like, but be honest, and don't be afraid to be vulnerable. Share your heart; write like nobody will ever read it. You can write anything you want dear one, but I have one requirement. You must end it with these words:

Your name is loved.

Your name is special.

Your name is precious.

Your name is beautiful.

Your name is seen.

Your name is fearfully and wonderfully made.

Now before you argue and write this assignment off, I ask that you do this, even if just for me. You don't even have to believe it, *yet*. It's okay if you don't, but I pray you will soon.

Till next time, Beautiful!

Eve

Things to Remember:

_____

_____

_____

_____

_____

_____

_____

_____

_____

_____

_____

_____

_____

_____

_____

Chapter 2
The Greatest Love Story

For God so loved the world that he gave his one and only Son, that whoever believes in him shall not perish but have eternal life.
John 3:16

Hello Beautiful,

What do you consider a great love story? Everyone

has in their mind what *"Happily Ever After"* looks like, but

what if we have it all wrong? Today I have something special

to share with you. I would like to challenge everything you

think you know about life and love. I know life hasn't been

easy. But hear me out, as I believe you are on the precipice

of realizing the greatest truth of all.

Many years ago, a beautiful love story was shared

with the world. Full of intrigue, romance and great courage, this story shares a message of encouragement, hope, and a plan of eternal love. This love story is a best-seller, and it's special because it is personal for every reader. In fact, it's a love letter written for those in whom the Creator breathed life. Inspired by the Author of love Himself. The One who is God and is Love in pure form. The Hero in this great love story is named *Jesus*, Son of the Living God.

⇨**Reflection Time:** What is your idea of a hero? There is so much media around us that gives us the world's idea of a hero, but once again, do we truly have it right? In your journal, write down all the characteristics you believe define a hero. ⇦

A verse in this story states, *"The thief comes only to steal and kill and destroy; I have come that they may have life, and have it to the full"* (John 10:10). I'd like to challenge you with a question: **What is life to the full for you?**

Another verse in the story gives us a clue: *"The fruit of the Spirit is love, joy, peace, forbearance (patience), kindness, goodness, faithfulness, gentleness and self-control* (Galatians 5:22-23). In just these two

> What is life to the full for you?

verses, we learn about three characters: Jesus, our hero, the thief, who is the enemy of our souls; and The Holy Spirit, our Helper, who is God in spirit form. As children of God, we receive His Spirit, who leads us to Jesus and blesses us with gifts or "fruit" when we walk with Him. Our Heavenly Father designed this fruit for us to experience a full life with Him by our side, whereas the enemy of our soul wants to take away everything that is good from us. Did you catch the part in John 10:10 where it says, *"I have come to give life?"* The truth is that our Hero, Jesus, **gave** His life so you could have life to the full- in addition to an eternity with Him. Talk about a full life!

But I'm getting ahead of myself. Shall we start

from the beginning?

***

Long ago, our Heavenly Father created the heavens and the earth. He breathed life into creation at the first moment in time, and His breath would become our own. In a personal moment blessed to us from the heart of the Father, we have the honor to peer through His eyes and witness His reflection in the beings He created in His Image. *"Very good,"* He said. Can you imagine this very first moment as He looked into the heart of man?

Our story continues as we familiarize ourselves with the first man and woman filled with the breath of life, Adam and Eve. And a new character enters our story: the serpent. Crafty and sly, he showed his colors as he twisted the words of God to our naive couple in the first lie ever told to humanity. Buying the lie of the enemy and consequently disobeying God's only command, Adam and Eve took their lives into their own hands. The result serving as a destructive consequence: the introduction of sin into their hearts and minds, a consequence we all pay the price for today.

⇨**Reflection Time:** It's important to understand that God did not create us as robots or puppets to fulfill His every whim. Instead, He created us for relationship with Him. This allows us the freedom to choose Him or to choose to follow our desires. Thankfully, Adam and Eve's choice, while tragic, was not the end of the story and does not have to be the end of our story either. ⇦

As time marched on, God revealed Himself to a man and instructed him to build an ark, as the world had become an evil place. God had to save the future of humanity from the enemy who had influenced man to disobey and ultimately to sin. So He chose Noah, a righteous man who walked faithfully with Him. After God saved Noah,

14

his family and select animals, He proceeded to destroy the rest of humanity.

⇨**Reflection Time:** This decision from a loving God has created great question in the minds of believers and nonbelievers alike. Why would a loving God choose to destroy the people He had created? We do not understand the mind of God, nor are we meant to, but we have to consider that God was protecting His creation from great evil that had infiltrated the hearts and minds of men.⇦

Our journey continues, as God chose Abraham to raise up a group of people who would become God's chosen, a people chosen to share His love and Word with a world who did not know their Creator. Jacob, Abraham's grandson, would raise twelve children who would become the twelve tribes of Israel. Moses would come later, chosen to lead these tribes out of slavery in Egypt. Hundreds of years later, God would inspire a young man named David, a man after God's own heart, to be King of his people. *(Remember David from my first letter?)* David would have a son named Solomon, who would become the wisest man of his age.

After Solomon, we begin to witness man go down a familiar road. Just as Adam and Eve chose to disobey God in the garden, we watch as God's chosen people turned away from Him again and again. So He sends prophets to remind them of his love. **Prophets such as:**

Isaiah, who proclaimed the coming of the Suffering Servant, the Savior and Messiah named Jesus (our Hero). Isaiah prophesied the salvation of Yahweh to God's people. (Book of Isaiah)

Jeremiah, was known as the weeping prophet because he was seemingly full of despair over the future. Jeremiah warned God's people about sin and judgement. (Book of Jeremiah)

Ezekiel reminded God's people of the sins that brought judgement while assuring them of the blessings of God's covenant. (Book of Ezekiel)

Daniel shared a prophetic word about the ultimate destiny of God's people. (Book of Daniel)

God would use many men and women alike to courageously serve as communicators between Him and His people during seasons when they chose not to listen to Him.

On each page, we see a beautiful thread woven through God's story as we witness persevering love in the heart of a Father towards those He shepherds. Just as a seamstress connects fabric within a patchwork quilt, God lovingly connects His creation to Himself through real stories of life and love that provide an opportunity for us to learn from God's perspective. In each story, we learn that God sees us, hears us and is with us. Check out a few of His stories of provision:

- Wisdom, as taught by Solomon in the book of **Proverbs**.
- Strength, worship and peace as shared by David in the book of **Psalms**.
- Perseverance as shown in **Nehemiah**, the one who rebuilt the great wall around Jerusalem in FIFTY-TWO DAYS!

- Courage as depicted through Gideon, in the book of **Judges**, the one named *"Mighty Warrior"* by an angel of God. Gideon would lead an army of 300 to face tens of thousands and WIN!
- The beauty of unconditional love as shown in the book of **Ruth**.
- Bravery to believe we were born for such a time as this as shown in the book of **Esther**.

Every story becomes a testimony of God's love and grace, and an opportunity to teach us how to have a better life. But you must know that each one points to a climax in The New Testament, when a young girl, just around your age, would be given a gift. Young Mary would deliver a baby wrapped in swaddling clothes and would name Him Jesus. *(Our Hero!)* Yes, the entire Old Testament tells us of the love of a Father for His people as He prepares them *(and us)* for the birth of His Son- the One who would bring an end to the power the evil one gained over our hearts the moment we bought his lie in the garden.

In the New Testament, we see the ministry of Jesus and His great love for us. He mentors twelve disciples while teaching those around Him to love God and people. Then the climactic pinnacle occurs when we read of his great sacrifice for us all, a sacrifice that would introduce redemption into the world.

⇨**Reflection Time:** What is redemption? Redemption is rescue and deliverance from sin. Why is redemption necessary? Remember how God had to destroy humanity in the days of Noah? The same enemy, who lied to Adam and Eve in the garden and lured humanity into evil, continues to distract and destroy those who choose not to allow God into their lives. He knows what we don't- sin takes us away from our Creator. Oh and by the way, it requires a debt to be paid at a very high interest rate. Much higher than we could ever afford. So God made a way for our debt to be paid through Jesus. When Jesus died, He took on the sins of all- past, present and future. His sacrifice served to restore us back to the Father. After three days, He resurrected and ascended into Heaven as our High Priest. And now, the enemy no longer has power to accuse us before the Father- unless we give it to Him. Once again, this is our choice.⇦

***

The New Testament continues with the church coming to life after Jesus resurrected and ascended to the right hand of God the Father. The church, created as an extension of the body of Jesus, was designed to continue His ministry and draw others to Him. This love story closes with the prophecy of the end of our age- Jesus' return, and the beautiful ending when we dwell with our God forever.

So why do I call this a love story? The One who created us loved us so much that He sent His one and only Son to die for us, so we could be with Him. *We* chose to walk away from Him, but *He* never gave up on us. His will was to reconcile us to Himself. But He had to make a way for that to happen. His *Unconditional love* is so much greater than the love stories of today, isn't it?

Now you must know this story has a purpose- that we would know our Father. He reveals Himself to us in creation and in his Word. But we must read it to know who He is truly. Proverbs 4:20-22 speaks to us, *"My son, pay attention to what I say; turn your ear to my words. Do not let them out of your sight, keep them within your heart; for they are life to those who find them and health to one's whole body."* No matter what we are going through, His Word, combined with prayer, nurtures a relationship with our Father- a relationship unlike any other. His Word mentors our hearts as He guides us past the distractions and challenges that feed our fear, worry, and insecurity. The enemy is still prowling around like a lion, but Jesus defeated the enemy at the cross, and we do not have to listen to or be afraid of Satan's lies. We can instead rest in the strength of our Savior.

Beautiful, remember free will? It is truly ours, but know that any choice comes with a consequence, good or bad. God knows that you are curious and are seeking answers. And the beauty of his Word, the Bible, is that it leads us to the One who answers our questions and helps

> You were made by Love to be Loved and to give Love

in any circumstance we face. To know God and His great love story, is to know the One who created you and loves you with all of His heart. Remember, He is with you through every challenge you face. You were made by the God of Love to be loved and to give love. When you know God and choose to follow His Son, you will begin to know who you are: ***His beloved daughter***.

When you don't know God, fear and worry can take a front seat. And if I may be transparent with you, my own life without God took a spiral downward when fear and worry took a front seat as I faced challenges. I'll share more on that in a future letter.

***

A Call to Action: Has your definition of Love changed? How about what defines a Hero? Continue to write down your thoughts in your journal. And over the next month, read one Psalm and one Proverb a day. Oh, and dig into the book of John; it's a beautiful reflection of the love of Jesus through the eyes of the disciple whom Jesus loved. Enjoy reading The Greatest Love Story ever written!

PS- Would you like to know Jesus? Check out page 192 for a

beautiful introduction to the One who gives life.

Love you, Beautiful!

Eve

Things to Remember:

_____

_____

_____

_____

_____

_____

_____

_____

_____

_____

_____

_____

_____

_____

_____

_____

Chapter 3
You are Beautiful

You will be a crown of splendor in the Lord's hand, a royal diadem in the hand of your God.
Isaiah 62:3

Hello Beautiful,

How are you doing today? You would never believe where

I am! I'm sitting in The North Georgia Mountains overlooking a slow

running river. It's a beautiful day in September. The trees above

cover me like a protective blanket as they reflect the sun on their

soft, green leaves. The birds are singing their morning song as geese

honk in the distance. The river leads to a small rapid about 200

yards downstream, and I hear refreshing water surging downhill,

defining the landscape surrounding it.

⇨**Reflection Time:** Close your eyes for a moment.

When you walk along a stream bed, what do you see? Do

you see messy fallen limbs sticking out of cold, dirty water?

Or do you see refreshing, life-giving water covering soft earth as oxygen-producing trees grow out of her depths?

Perspective is everything. ⇦

Dry your tears, Beautiful. Yes, you are beautiful. I know, people may have said otherwise. You've allowed negative words to penetrate your heart, haven't you? But the bully doesn't know what I know, that your heart, just like this river, is a never ending supply of life to those around you.

> Perspective is everything.

You see, God uses your heart to pour life into others. I know you tire of hearing that beauty is on the inside, but it's true. *Your heart, just like this river, becomes a tributary of love to those God places in your path.*

What is beauty? You've heard the quote, "Beauty is in the eye of the beholder?" It's important to recognize *who* your beholder is because this is the person who will define beauty **for you**. I won't spoil my next letter, but we must take a moment to consider the voices that speak into us about beauty. Who is right, and who is wrong? There are many different opinions on the matter, and trust me, the voice you choose to listen to *matters*. Dear one, I want you to hear this straight from me: the only opinion that matters is that of the One who created you. God made you in His image, and therefore, you are beautiful in His eyes. Yep, Genesis 1:27 states, *"So God created mankind in his own image, in the image of God he created them; male and female he created them."* Genesis 1:31 continues, *"God saw all that he had made, and it was very good."* We are beautiful because the One who defined beauty in the first place made us. Not only did He make us, but He made us in His image and called us good!

God created beauty. He created us and placed something very special within us. Peter describes it like this, *"Rather, it should be that of your inner self, the unfading beauty of a gentle and quiet spirit, which is of great worth in God's sight"* (1 Peter 3:4). When God looks at us, He sees our heart. He sees the gentle and quiet spirit within us. When God looks at us- He sees Jesus. Our reflection in God's eyes reveals the spirit of Jesus, and this is of great worth to

Him. Isaiah relates our worth to that of royalty when he shares that God's children would be a *"crown of splendor- a royal diadem"* (Isaiah 62:3). A royal diadem is a crown, and in this reference, we cannot miss the significance of the beauty and royalty Isaiah placed on God's children. Consider this for a moment: our Abba Father calls His children beautiful. And as His children we are royalty, adopted into His family. Yes, *you,* dear one, are a beautiful princess in the eyes of your Heavenly Father.

Now with that said, we must have the hard conversations on value and self-image. As we dig into these topics, may I ask that you put away your mirror for a moment and recognize that reflections of beauty are three-dimensional? If I were to hold a two-dimensional mirror to this three-dimensional landscape in front of me, I would never capture every detail. Not even a photograph can capture the intricate design of every article in my gaze. Just so, mirrors and cameras cannot capture every detail of beauty within us either.

Hmm, why do we rely on them so much?

As we continue, I will introduce you to some incredible young women who have crossed my path. I have to tell you that the cool part in my journey is that just as God pours life into them through me, He also pours life into *me* through *them*. Allow me to introduce you to each of them as I share various topics in remaining letters. I know they will encourage you just as they have me.

Are you ready? Let's do this!

***

VALUE

Where do you find value? Where do you find *your* value? I know, it's easy to seek your value in the eyes of those who surround you, but is that truly where your value lies? What if that person leaves? Does your value change?

Take a dollar bill. A dollar is always a dollar. The beholder can not redefine the economic value of a dollar as less than the predefined value. In other words, even when it changes hands, a dollar doesn't change value.

But how often do we place our value into the hands of others, only to find ourselves disappointed when they don't recognize our worth? Do they really have the power to devalue us? My friend Katelyn has something to say on the subject:

> "It's easy to find our value in the eyes of others, but this view often becomes distorted. The reflection in the mirror becomes clear when I look at myself as God sees me, recognizing that my value comes from Him, not from others."

Such great advice! The voices we listen to shape us. Do we listen to the voice of the mean boy on the bus or do we listen to the heart of the One who created us?

***

SELF-IMAGE

Webster's dictionary describes *"image"* using words like, "appearance, reflection, idea, conception." All these words point to a picture. Add the word "self" to "image," and essentially the definition becomes the picture that we have of self. Let's think about pictures. I don't know about you, but when I take a picture I cannot capture the depth of my subject. So how can a picture describe who we are? Way too often, we allow pictures to define us and in turn define our self-image.

My friend, Moriah, would like to debunk this picture:

*"**S**ociety draws a picture, but it isn't real. It doesn't jump off the page. **YOU ARE REAL!**"*

You Are
Real!

You ***are*** real. Go ahead, Girl, say the words out loud, *"I AM REAL!"* Dear one, I may try to capture your depths within a photograph, but it's impossible. Why? Because you, Girl, jump off the page. You are real! Sing it, shout it out, dance in the freedom of this truth remembering that ***nobody*** can take this truth from you!

Emma, another of my friends, says:

*"**W**e often become obsessed with allowing our self-image to shape into a "certain type of person" based on external influences. We go after who we think we **should be** all the while denying who we truly are. We MUST avoid contemplating our self-worth and calculating what others see in us. Instead we must recognize who God says we are, and in this we find our true colors."*

These are some pretty powerful words. Chasing after someone you were never meant to be is like chasing fireflies. You may capture the light for a moment but choosing not to surrender it to the natural could smother the beautiful light within. When we box ourselves into a seemingly perfect package based on external influence, we are smothering the light God placed within us. It's time to surrender to the natural. See yourself as God sees you.

***

But I'm a hot mess. How can I be beautiful?

My friend Morgan wants you to know,

> "It's in your smile. Your smile attracts others to you. When you smile, you shine, and your eyes reflect what is in your heart. Your smile is contagious as it reflects the joy inside of you. I know it sounds cliché, but it truly is what's on the inside that makes you beautiful!"

***

But why don't people like me?

How do you know they don't? People love you. Maybe you don't hear it enough, but they do. My friend, Candace wants you to know this:

> "*I get it, we hear negative words that influence our inner thoughts- words such as: ugly, stupid, annoying, and crazy. But you see, you have the power to accept or reject these words. Those words should never impact your view of yourself; instead allow them to turn negative into positive. Ask, "How can I learn from this?" If there is nothing to learn from those words, throw them away.*"

***

But I have "(Insert issue here)."

I know you struggle, Beautiful. You struggle with insecurity, worry, fear and anxiety. But please listen. These do not define you! Candace shares that:

> "*It's okay not to be okay. It's okay to have issues, to be stressed out, to feel frustrated, but you can't allow the negative things in your life to consume you. You must know that you have the strength within you to get through the struggles you face.*"

Are you listening to these beautiful words? This type of freedom is worth celebrating via a dance in the rain! You don't have to be perfect. And you don't have to let your struggle consume you; in fact, you have the strength to face your struggles and say NOT TODAY!

But don't I need others' approval?

Beautiful, if you wait for others approval, you will be waiting a long time, forever even. My friend Jada says,

> "*We will never find the affirmation we seek through others. If you want to experience true love, fall on your knees before the Lord. True Love means the Cross. True Love looks like this: As messy as my life is, as ugly as it is, despite my being mediocre in a thousand things; Jesus came to die for me and to know me intimately. Love from others is conditional. With Jesus, there are no strings attached, because He loves us unconditionally.*"

Jada wants you to look at the reflection in the mirror, smile, and see the spark within yourself. Consider this reflection of a spark in Numbers 6:25 as God speaks to Moses a blessing for his people, *"The Lord will make his face shine upon you."*

The Lord created us in His Image- the image of Almighty God, the One who makes His face to shine upon us, the One who looks at His children and sees His Son Jesus. He sees us with unveiled face as we are transformed into His Image. **Do you see it?**

But does God even SEE ME?

YES! Now it's my turn for a word of encouragement.

*"**D**id you know that the night before Jesus was arrested, He prayed a prayer over you? A paraphrase from John 17:21, 'I pray for those who believe in Me, that all of them will be one, Father, just as You are in Me and I am in You.' To be one is to be whole, to be known, to be seen. Beautiful, when you say yes to Jesus you become one with Him, the One who sees you! Read John 17 and hear Him as He intercedes for you."*

I invite you to join me at the riverbank. Close your eyes and breathe in the fresh air. Hear the softly rolling water. Sit in the presence of the Father and see yourself through His Eyes.

> See yourself through the Father's Eyes

***

A Call to Action: Listen to "Beautiful" by MercyMe. Write down the verses shared in this letter. I encourage you to open God's Word and find His truth about beauty through His Eyes.

Until my next letter,

I Love you, Beautiful!

Eve

Things to Remember:

_____

_____

_____

_____

_____

_____

_____

_____

_____

_____

_____

_____

_____

_____

_____

Chapter 4
Who Defines You?

*See what great love the Father has lavished on us, that we should be called **children of God**! And that is what we are! The reason the world does not know us is that it did not know him.*
1 John 3:1

Hello Beautiful,

Happy hump day! Here's a little Bible trivia. Did you know

the sun and the moon were created on the fourth

day? Wednesday, the fourth day, is Hump Day because by the end

of the day we have officially gotten over the *hump* of the work

week. Do you think God thought He was officially *"over the hump"*

in creation after He had created the sun and the moon? Maybe this

is why the *humpback* whale arrived on day five? Oh and let's not

forget the one and two *hump* camels on day six. Oh, my imagination

is quite colorful. I believe God has a wonderful sense of humor. And

I know there will come a day when we will be able to hear all of His amazing stories of creation first hand and ask any questions that we may have.

So, how is your day going, Beautiful? What did you think of my last letter? I know that you struggle with self-image, but please **NEVER** forget how beautiful you are.

Can you do me a favor? I want you to write down the verse I sent you in my first letter, Psalm 139:13-14. Write it down and place it on your mirror. You see, I have learned over time that gentle DAILY reminders allow God to write His truth on our hearts. So write it, read it, commit it to memory. Remember, this is His love story written to and for you.

Don't you find it interesting that we find ways to re-define things over time? Hump day is a fun way to define the middle of the week, especially when you're looking forward to Friday. However, we must take great care with redefining things that already have a definition.

So who defines *you*?

Time for transparency!

I remember my excitement to enter middle school. I had an intense desire to be somebody I wasn't. And while my best friend loved me just as I was, I found it hard to believe due to years of feeling unloved. Hindsight will not allow me to forget the blonde attempt that turned into an obtrusive shade of orange. And then there was the blue eyeshadow (Ugh, why didn't somebody tell me that blue is NOT a good color for me?) Let's not forget my unhealthy desire to own a pair of Jordache jeans. Then there's the memory of how much I hated my shape because I longed to look like the girl on the cover of *Seventeen Magazine*. Today my heart cries for the girl who thought she had finally found a love interest, only to realize that his interest wasn't in her heart.

Who defines you?

Can you relate to any of these? Do you also struggle with feeling unloved, uncertain of who you are, and finding yourself in the comparison trap?

In the same letter that declares you fearfully and wonderfully made, God speaks the following truths that I don't want you to miss. He declares that *"you are beautiful"* (Ecclesiastes 3:11). He *"created you in his image"* (Genesis 1:27). He says, *"You are loved"* (John 3:16).

And for those who follow Jesus (let me introduce you-p192), He has declared *"you a new creation"* (2 Corinthians 5:17) and He has said, *"You are a temple"* (1 Corinthians 3:16). He defines you as *"a child of God"* (1 John 3:1). He has said, *"you are his daughter"* (2 Corinthians 6:18). And He wants you to know *"you are CHOSEN"* (1 Peter 2:9). I encourage you to write these truths down, allow *The Great I Am* to write them on your heart.

In this challenging age, so many influences around us beg the question, *"Who am I?"* Since we have read what God has said about it, let's chat about what the world says for a moment, shall we? I shared the trap of comparison that led to my insecurity over the girl on the cover of *Seventeen Magazine.* Do you ever find yourself in a similar place? Virtual social media feeds lure us into a false sense of comparison, don't they? Likes and comments raise our desire to compete. Scrolling through perfect poses encourages us to see through the lens the world supplies. "She lives the perfect life and therefore I too must live the perfect life," the world claims. But here's the thing, virtual reality is all too- well virtual. It isn't real.

Virtual reality is all too- virtual

So, let's peer behind the camera for a moment, shall we? The girl in the post is just like you- she goes to school. She hangs out with friends. But would you be surprised to know that she struggles with insecurity? The girl in the video has parents who remind her to do homework and finish chores. Would it shock you to know that she too experiences anxiety, fear and thoughts that lead to worry? So, we have to ask the question, **can a perfect pose reflect a real life**?

Next, I think we should broach other's expectations. God has placed people around you who will both influence you and be influenced by you. And I'd like to encourage you that this is by design. In fact, Proverbs 13:20 instructs, *"Walk with the wise and become wise, for a companion of fools suffers harm."* So it is by design that we walk alongside others who will influence and therefore have expectations of us. But this knowledge bears the question, *"Do their expectations on our lives define us or can we recognize that in fact, there is a refining process going on?"*

How about the girl at school who makes fun of you? Does she truly know the real you? I wonder if she shares in your fear? Her reaction may be a bit different from yours, but I wonder if there is a deeper issue going on here. While she calls you names, I would like you to consider that perhaps this is all she knows. Until we've walked in her shoes, we never really know her struggle. May I suggest that we should never allow our insecurity, and other's negative expectations or course words to define what God has already defined. However, perhaps there is something else going on; perhaps we are being *"refined"* through the process? Beautiful, please know that nobody can redefine what God has defined; however, I feel it necessary to share a hard truth with you- God will allow others to refine you, which leads me to my next point.

***

Refining or defining?

One of the most encouraging people in my life has been my BFF. She never allowed me to sit in the mire of insecurity, but instead always encouraged me to see myself through her eyes. God gave me a beautiful gift in my friend, Lisa. We welcome those who lift us up, don't we? Do you have someone who serves to lift you up?

But what if I told you that even those who discourage and disappoint serve a purpose in your refinement?

Consider a diamond: what you see in the store is the result of a great refining process. The process of transformation begins 100 miles underground in a state of great heat and pressure. Scientists say diamonds reached the earth's surface many years ago through a volcanic eruption. The rocks found at the bottom of kimberlite pipes are blasted through mining. The journey of the rock continues through a process of crushing and milling. The rough diamond is separated from the dust then sorted and separated for cutting before reaching the final process of polishing. Wow, the diamond goes through a lot before making her way to the store product case, doesn't she?

Every step of this process, while stressful as it may seem, is critical in the forming of the diamond. The processing of this gem includes heat, pressure, eruption, blasting, crushing, milling, sorting, cutting, shaping and polishing. These processes all work together to prepare this intricate gem for her destination. In our own journey, God

> God defined you.

prepares us through seasons of refining that often include people who create pressure or make us feel pressure. This begs the question, *"Does refining serve to define us?"*

My friend Samuel wants you to know this:

> *"**G**od defines you as valuable, more valuable than anything on earth. He sees you as a gem, yet He doesn't love anyONE more than the others. He doesn't define you as just another in His collection, but as you are, beautiful, unique, His precious child."*

God defined you. WOW! Read Samuel's words aloud, now close your eyes and consider this truth: **you are special.** The same

One who placed the Sun and Moon in the sky, the One who perfectly positioned every star, The Creator *Elohim*, defined you. He may allow others to refine you, and often under pressure. But He has already defined you as beautiful, unique and valuable in His eyes. He encourages us to live confident in this truth- even as others may attempt to speak otherwise. Beautiful, nobody can redefine what He has defined. He has the first and the last word, so we must protect that which He has defined, *"Above all else, guard your heart, for everything you do flows from it"* (Proverbs 4:23).

There is a gem tucked within God's love story in Judges 6. The Israelites, God's chosen people, had turned away from the Lord and were oppressed by the Midianites. In their distress, they cried out to the Lord to help them. His response:

"The angel of the Lord came and sat down under the oak in Ophrah that belonged to Joash the Abiezrite, where his son Gideon was threshing wheat in a winepress to keep it from the Midianites. When the angel of the Lord appeared to Gideon, he said, 'The Lord is with you, mighty warrior.'

'Pardon me, my lord but if the Lord is with us, why has all this happened to us? Where are all his wonders that our ancestors told us about when they said, 'Did not the Lord bring us up out of Egypt?' But now the Lord has abandoned us and given us into the hand of Midian.' The Lord turned to him and said, 'Go in the strength you have and save Israel out of Midian's hand. Am I not sending you?' 'Pardon me my Lord,' Gideon replied, 'but how can I save Israel? My clan is the weakest in Manasseh, and I am the least in my family.'"

⇨**Reflection Time:** I LOVE this story for so many reasons, but mostly because it's a beautiful example of a perfect God who stands outside of space and time, reaching down to meet us where we are in all of our insecurity.⇦

Do you ever find yourself in a place like Gideon- hiding under the false "not good enough" rock? Let me explain Gideon's plight:

Gideon was living in the time of the Judges, a dark time of Israel's history when they had turned away from God and considered themselves *"right in their own eyes"* (Judges 21:25). The Midianites were so oppressive Judges 6:2-4 says, that *"the Israelites prepared shelters for themselves in mountain clefts, caves and strongholds. Whenever the Israelites planted their crops, the Midianites, Amalekites and other eastern peoples invaded the country, camping on the land and ruining the crops all the way to Gaza, not sparing a living thing for Israel, neither sheep nor cattle nor donkeys."* I wonder, do you think God was allowing the Midianites to refine his chosen people?

We find Gideon essentially hiding from the pressure created by turmoil in his country. But his family still needed to eat, so Gideon was threshing wheat (or beating stalks of grain to separate the kernels of grain from the chaff) in a winepress that was probably just a pit, made out of rock or lined with plaster and used to trample grapes to make wine.

So Almighty God, *El Shaddai,* reached down into a dark period of history. Not only did He reach, but the Word says the angel of the Lord "sat down" and the first thing he says to Gideon is,

"The Lord is with you, mighty warrior." Doesn't this give you chills?

Can you imagine? But Gideon, not quite seeing the moment as I see

it, is arguing with the angel even to the point of complaining that

the Lord had abandoned them. But what does the angel say? *"Go in*

the strength you have and save Israel out of Midian's hand. Am I not

sending you?" Gideon replies *"How can I save Israel? My clan is the*

weakest in Manasseh and I am the least in my family."

Was Gideon mistaking refining for defining? Let's take a

deeper look:

1- The angel says, *"The Lord is with you,"* and Gideon replies

*"**BUT IF** the Lord is with us **WHY** has this happened to us, well He*

***MUST HAVE** abandoned us."* Gideon was so caught up in the

current circumstance around him that he allowed the "but's," "if's,"

"why's," and "must have's" to distract him from God's truth. Don't

we do this too? How often do we allow our circumstances to

determine our rejection? Is it really that hard to believe that we *are*

chosen?

2- The angel called Gideon a *"Mighty Warrior"* and told him that he was being sent to save Israel. But Gideon once again argues, *"**BUT HOW** can I save Israel? My clan is the **WEAK**est in Manasseh, and **I AM** the **LEAST** in my family."* Gideon allowed the opinions of society to crush him before he ever had a chance to be formed. Oh dear one, how many times have you allowed others' opinions spoken about you to crush your spirit?

But wait, forming the diamond is a process, right?

Hear my heart, Beautiful. God hears all of our excuses, complaints and misconceptions, yet He still sits with us and listens. I am certain in that moment the Lord looked at Gideon with love as He said, *"I will be with you, and you will strike down all the Midianites, leaving none alive."*

Dear one, no matter where you are or what pressure you find yourself under, God is ALWAYS with you. While He may allow refining to take place to grow you, His definition of who you are never changes and He **will** attempt to debunk the misconceptions you have allowed to enter your heart.

Are you listening to Him?

49

God debunked all of Gideon's assumptions and misconceptions of who he thought he was with two words, *"Mighty Warrior."* Then God challenged him with a great task as He encouraged with this promise, *"I will be with you."*

> Mighty Warrior- God is with you.

Beautiful, allow me to encourage you with this truth: Just as He called Gideon "Mighty Warrior," He calls you that too. And just as He was with Gideon, He is with you.

Now, I won't ruin the rest of the story for you, but I encourage you to go read all of Judges 6 for yourself. It's quite exciting!

***

So what does God say about you?

My friend Samuel has more to say on this matter:

> *"God counted all of the hairs on your head and considers you more valuable than even the birds of the air."*

Look up, dear one. What do you see? We have a flock of

geese living just behind our house that I delight in commuting to work alongside. There's just something about seeing this beautiful family in perfect formation that reminds me of the truth of God's provision in action. Just as Samuel reminds us, Matthew 6:26 tells us, *"Look at the birds of the air, they do not sow or reap or store away in barns, and yet your heavenly Father feeds them. Are you not much more valuable than they?"* I believe our Father is reminding us of His provision- if they are valuable, we are even more valuable. Do you see what I see when you look up? Even if you don't, keep looking. And remember every time He looks down- He sees you.

My friend Rachel, wants you to know this:

"God defined who we are and how much He loves us. When He looks at us, His sons and daughters, God sees His beloved Son, Jesus. God shares this truth with us in His Word, the Bible, truth that does not change. There is nothing we can say or do to change His Word."

Wow, what a beautiful gift! We look at ourselves in the mirror and see a two-dimensional image, but when our Father looks at us, He sees His perfect three-dimensional Son reflected in our uniquely created hearts. With her encouragement, my friend reminds me of the reflection in the river with the sunlight beaming overhead. Dear one, if you remember nothing else please remember this: **Your Heavenly Father, the Creator of the universe, defined you as His daughter- a child of God, beautiful, created in His Image, loved, a new creation, a temple, chosen and valuable.** Who is anyone else to say otherwise?

***

A Call to Action before our next letter: Take some index cards, write down the defining verses from this chapter. Include your name in place of the words "you" and "I." Then place them on your mirror where they are readily visible. Believe this truth from your Heavenly Father. Beautiful, He wrote them for you.

Love you,

Until our next letter,

Eve

Things to Remember:

_____

_____

_____

_____

_____

_____

_____

_____

_____

_____

_____

_____

_____

_____

_____

Chapter 5
You have a Purpose

For I know the plans I have for you, declares the Lord, plans to prosper you and not to harm you, plans to give you hope and a future.
Jeremiah 29:11

Hello, Beautiful!

Did you miss me? I've been thinking about you. I've been

excited to see how you are coming along with collecting God's

reminders. I pray that *El Elyon,* God most High, is opening your

heart to who He is and who you are while growing you in the

process.

As I consider your growth, I stand amazed at the power of

our Creator, His promises, the strength He is building within you

and the comfort He gives in your moments of uncertainty. Yes, I

know you struggle, dear one, and in this letter I would like to

encourage you to face your uncertainty over these eight

unanswered questions found on your heart. Are you ready?

1. *"I'm not (insert reason here) enough to have purpose."*

2. *"How long do I have to wait?"*

3. *"How do I know what God wants me to choose?"*

4. *"I'm afraid of the unknown."*

5. *"What if I fail?"*

6. *"What if people disagree with my choice?"*

7. *"I just don't know what I want to be when I grow up."*

8. *"What if I choose wrong?"*

Can I share with you that even though I'm thirty years older than you, today, I too stand at a great crossroads? Faced with a decision that will change everything in my life, I am learning this truth: **Life brings many challenges that create moments of tension. These can lead us to question if we are on the right path.** I'd like to encourage you to embrace this tension and recognize you have a great purpose and a Father who wants to lead you on the path He has designed.

Remember studying photosynthesis? How cool it is to see

things grow. Let's take a look through the magnifying glass:

- A seed is planted.
- Water falls to earth and nourishes the seed, which explodes into life.
- Roots begin to form, spreading out into the surrounding soil.
- *And all of this is underground, not visible to our naked eye!*
- A stem begins to peek through the soil as it stretches to the sun.
- You begin to see the branches form from the stem.
- A little bud appears.
- A flower blooms, and fruit appears.
- Bees pollinate, spreading the seed from the bloom which starts the process again.

Do you see it? Every part of this process serves a special

purpose. But, imagine these scenarios:

What if the seed decided it didn't want to come out of the shell?

Or if the water said, *"I don't want to nourish the soil. I want to go play in the swimming pool."*

What if the roots complained, *"There's a rock in the way, what do we do now?"*

Or how about if the bloom said, *"I don't think I want to open today. Can't I just sleep all day?"*

Sound silly? But how often have you asked similar

questions?

***

But I'm not (*List reason here*):

If every part of a plant's growth has a purpose, what about you? I know there are people who have said you aren't good enough, old enough, pretty enough, even smart enough. But what if they're wrong? God says, *For I know the plans I have for you, plans to prosper you and not to harm you, plans to give you hope and a future* (Jeremiah 29:11 paraphrased).

Yes, I know, there are times when you just want to sleep in, times you're afraid of what others will think, and other times when you just don't know what to do. But consider the plant- every level of growth serves the purpose of maturing as the plant reaches for God's great design. Don't allow fear, insecurity or even laziness to create a barrier preventing you from going after the Creator's plan for your life. If He calls you to it, He will see you through it.

***

But when does my purpose begin?

God has given you a purpose, and He wants to give you hope. He has a future designed just for you, but that doesn't mean you can merely sit still and watch Him work.

My friend Rachel has something to say on this topic:

> "**G**od has blessed you with gifts that, when used, will help you succeed, bring Him glory, and encourage others in their faith. Today your purpose may be to get up, go to school, or even serve your family. Tomorrow, God may place a desire on your heart to learn something new. The gifts He has given will align with the desires of your heart as He provides you the strength to complete your designed purpose."

It has been said that purpose keeps us focused and constant on our journey, it's the engine that drives our life and leadership. Once we have a purpose, we give it effort and focus. Notice that purpose is described in the present tense, meaning that we have purpose every day of our lives. If God counted all of our days, then it stands to reason that He has given you purpose TODAY! With this knowledge, we all need to understand that with today's purpose comes choice.

***

How do I know what God wants me to choose?

My friend Dusti has a great analogy to share with you:

"Let's say God has offered you two kinds of ice cream- chocolate or strawberry, your choice. You can choose either or nothing. But you must choose. Oh and choosing nothing? Yes, that too is a choice."

> How do I know what to choose?

In Dusti's analogy, God offers strawberry and chocolate with the option to choose either. Chocolate may be your favorite, but strawberry is just as good of an option. The nutritional information directs you how much to eat. If you eat the per-serving amount of either choice, then you will meet the nutritional requirements as you enjoy a tasty treat. However, if you eat too much, you'll step outside the boundary given and could face the consequence of an expanding waistline. If you eat none, then you'll not enjoy the gift at all.

You see, God gave you "free will" when He formed you. The Father isn't a puppet-master telling you how to live your life; however, He recognizes that we face choices every day, so he gave us a guide. God's love letter gives us direction, highlighting the good and the bad, while declaring boundaries that keep us safe from much more than an expanding waistline. If we choose to step outside His boundaries, then we face consequences. But if we step out in faith and accept our purpose, while staying inside the boundaries given; then we have the opportunity to not only enjoy His gift, but also experience His love through relationship as He guides us through His Word.

⇨**Reflection Time:** Speaking of His love letter, have you started reading it? Come on now, don't procrastinate. He has so much to share with you and has taken the first step; now it's your turn. Go on, pick up his Word to learn more about who He is and how much He cares for you. He is waiting with outstretched arms to take you on a grand adventure!⇦

***

But I'm afraid of the unknown:

Every day carries with it a challenge. But guess what? **A challenge is nothing more than a hill to climb. You may not see the top for the clouds, but once you've reached it, you'll be able to look back and recognize that the journey was far greater than the excitement of completion.** I'll save challenges for a future letter, but for now let's chat about the unknown. Rachel mentioned daily purposes: *"to get up, go to school or serve your family."* The specific tasks that make these up may include brushing your teeth, doing your homework, cleaning your room or doing the dishes (to name a few). You know about these because they are routine, and dare I say predictable? But can you find purpose in these: the pop quiz, the conflict, the loved one who gets sick, the parent who leaves or the friend who chooses to walk away? Where do you find your purpose when you're faced with the unpredictable?

⇨**Reflection Time:** I know Beautiful, some of these

are heavy. To be honest, my first reaction when I've faced a heavy unknown has been to get angry, run, hide, or even worse, to allow fear's grip to paralyze me into indecision and inaction. So if you will, please allow me to take your hand as we face the unknown together. ⇦

I feel the need to say this out loud, "**The unknown is inevitable.**" Now you say it, "**The unknown is inevitable.**" Now say it three times fast, **"The unknown is inevitable."** Come now, I think we need to embrace this together!

The brothers of Jesus knew a little something about the unknown. John 7 gives us a reflection of what James and his brothers thought of Jesus in the early years: *"For even his own brothers did not believe in him"* (John 7:5). Historians believe they thought Jesus was crazy. I can only imagine the challenges experienced by the brothers of the Son of God. Do you think they were always asking, *"What will He do next?"* Can you relate with James? We don't get to choose our siblings, do we?

When I think about how the brother of Jesus went from

thinking He was crazy, to sharing Jesus' teachings as the leader of the Jerusalem Christian Church, I want to sit down with this man for a chat. What would you ask Him, if given the chance? I would ask, "What changed, James? When did you decide to go all in and believe?" Theologians believe it was the resurrection of Jesus that changed his heart. Can you imagine what his conversion must have been like? Perhaps it changed him so much that he later defined himself as a servant of Jesus in verse 1 of the epistle he wrote? *Wait a second, his brother is now his servant?* Wow, what a change of heart! Perhaps one day, James will share with us the experience that led to his declaration, *"Whenever you face trials..."* (James 1:2a). The emphasis here is on "WHEN." I think James knew first hand, with a brother like Jesus, that life isn't supposed to be easy! *(But who ever said it would be?)*

Solomon, David's son, gave us clear instruction that applies to embracing the unknown: *"Trust in the Lord with all your heart and lean not on your own understanding; in all your ways submit to him, and he will make your paths straight"* (Proverbs 3:5-6). It's easy to trust God when life is going our way, but when an unknown occurs, how do we trust what we can't see?

*"Only in the **leap** from the lion's head will he prove his worth."*[1] In *Indiana Jones and The Last Crusade*, Indy faced many unknowns as he sought the Holy Grail, but it was a ***leap of faith*** that proved to be my favorite. While Indy was following a map to the grail- he met with a scary unknown as he faced a canyon with no bridge. It was only by faith or "trust" that Indy could move forward. In the moment when it counted most, Indy showed us where our purpose lies as we too face the unknown. As he closed his eyes and placed one foot forward, a wooden path appeared! Now, I am in no way suggesting you follow Indy's footsteps over a pathless canyon; however, I believe his action gives an example of how you will find your purpose in the unknown. Trust and step out in faith with one foot in front of the other.

***

---

[1] http://www.imdb.com/title/tt0097576/quotes

But what if I fail?

I wish I could tell you that failure isn't an option. We hear this message often in our lives, wouldn't you agree? But the truth is that we will have moments when we don't meet the mark. Just as we face trials, we will also face failure. It is our reaction to failure, however, that is important.

> The only true failure is when you fail to try.

Rosemarie encourages us:

*"**D**on't be afraid to fail."*

Wow, and there it is! You may receive a failing grade on your math pop quiz, but you have a choice to fall back and worry over what has already taken place or fail forward and develop stronger study habits. Failure isn't an obstacle, but an opportunity. **And the only true failure is when you fail to try.** The earlier we accept this and choose to learn from it, the more prepared we are to face difficult challenges in life.

So, my dear, toss the covers off, get up, stretch and face the day! He only expects you to live one day and take one step at a time with Him by your side. And if you fail, He will pick you up and give you the strength to keep going.

***

But what will others think of me? What if they disagree with my choice?

Remember the story of David? I have often asked the question, *"How did he beat a seven-foot giant when he was only a boy?"* In his challenge, he was angry because this giant was insulting God's army. He recognized Goliath had to be taken down as he said to Saul, *"Let no one lose heart on account of this Philistine; your servant will go and fight him"* (1 Samuel 17:32). In response to Saul's reply, *"You are only a young man,"* David says, *"The Lord who rescued me from the paw of the lion and the paw of the bear will rescue me from the hand of this Philistine"* (1 Samuel 17:37). Without armor or an arsenal of weapons, he chose five smooth stones and a slingshot. Trusting God to give him the courage,

strength and wisdom needed to win the battle, David didn't shy

away. And God rewarded him with victory!

Catch two things in this story.

1. David didn't allow Saul's opinion to stop him from

pursuing his purpose.

Beautiful not only will others try to re-define who you are,

but they may also try to tell you what you

should or should not do in life. The

> You can't aim for your goals if you aim to please

question is not *if* others disagree with

your choice, but **when.** Here's the

bottom line, they don't have to reach

your goals or face the outcome, only you do. **And you can't aim for**

your goals if you aim to please. The freedom of free will is this: **you**

get to make the choice.

2. David went into battle prepared, trusting God to protect

him. A promise given many years after this battle gives us some

insight into his great faith. David lived out what Paul would later teach: *I can do all things through Christ who strengthens me (Philippians 4:13 paraphrased).* David knew that when God gives you a purpose, He doesn't expect you to complete it on your strength or merit. Instead He **expects** you to ask Him for help and He **promises** to help you. So shed the opinions of others dear one and seek what God has to say about the matter.

***

But I don't know what my purpose is.

Our society places a great deal of pressure on you to know where you are going in life, but the honest truth is that we do not know the future, only God does. We can pray for God to give us wisdom. We can seek to define and enhance our strengths and weaknesses. We can search for the things in life that bring us joy, but only God knows our future, and He does not want us to get stuck in the quicksand of *what if* and *when.*

Dear one, my friend Jenna has something to say about this:

"It's okay if you don't know what He has planned for your

life just yet. There have been times I too have questioned the choices I've made, but at the end of the day I realize that when I keep my focus on Him and not on the plan for my life, it becomes more about the journey than the end result. He may not reveal everything to me in the next minute, day, or year even, but He will reveal it when I am ready to receive it."

Yes, dear one, it is okay. That is why you have a lifetime, right? I love how Joyce Meyer says this in her book *Hearing from God each Morning,*

"People often wonder, 'What am I supposed to do with my life? What is my purpose for being alive?' One way that God answers these questions is through our natural gifts and abilities. He leads us to understand our purpose through the skills and talents He gives us. A God-given talent, or what we often call "a gift," is something we can do easily, something that comes naturally. For example, many great artists know just how to put shapes and colors together, so they enjoy painting, sculpting, or designing buildings. Many songwriters hear music in their heads, and they simply write down these melodies and lyrics to make beautiful music. Some people have natural abilities to organize or administer, while others are gifted as counselors, helping people sort out their lives and relationships. No matter what our talents are, we derive great pleasure from doing what we are naturally good at doing. If you are not sure of your purpose in life, just do what you are good at and then watch God confirm your choices by blessing your endeavors. If we do what we are good at doing, we will sense God's anointing (presence and power) on our efforts. We will know we are operating in our gifts

and that doing so honors God and ministers life to others."[2]

Isn't that good? So what do I hear from this amazing advice? **God has called us to live in the chapter of today. Do what you are good at, and in His perfect timing, He will prepare you for the chapter of tomorrow.**

Check out His promise in 2 Peter 1:3-4a: *"His divine power has given us everything we need for a godly life through our knowledge of him who called us by his glory and goodness. In these, God has given us his very great and precious promises, so that through them you may participate in the divine nature."*

> God has called us to live in the chapter of today.

Beautiful, standing on this promise allows you to see His fingerprints interwoven throughout each page of your life.

***

But what if I choose wrong?

---

[2] Hearing from God Each Morning- 365 Devotions- Joyce Meyer

What if you do? Every season of our life has a purpose, and there is something to be learned in every challenge, both large and small. Even if we choose chocolate when strawberry was the better choice, God redeems that choice and will use it for your good and His glory. But I will save that for another day. Until our next letter, be encouraged with this passage:

"As the rain and snow come down from heaven, and do not return to it without nourishing the earth to provide seed for the sower and bread for the eater, so my Word will not return to me without performing the purpose for which I sent it" (Isaiah 55:10-12).

Just as photosynthesis highlights God's great design in the flower, this scripture promises that His purpose will prevail in all things, *including you*. He will nourish you, provide the foundation for your roots to grow, give you the strength to stretch through the unknown, furnish resources so you can step into the purpose He has for you, and delight as you bloom in the purpose He designed uniquely for you. And as a bonus, He draws you near to Him as you learn to trust Him. Your growth brings Him glory as you shine His

light on others to do the same.

***

A Call to Action: In your journal write down your dreams

and goals, both short and long term.

> Don't focus on
> the destination
> Focus on the
> journey

Under each one, list the steps

needed to achieve these goals. Don't

stress over it; just write at least one

line for each. Pray for God's wisdom to align you with His will. Then

begin, one step at a time. Don't focus on the destination, but on the

journey. And if you get waylaid on your journey, no worries; just re-

align with the One who gave you life. Your plans will carry you on a

lifetime journey toward God's purpose.

Well, I'm off to find some chocolate ice cream.

Love you, Beautiful!

Eve

Things to Remember:

_____

_____

_____

_____

_____

_____

_____

_____

_____

_____

_____

_____

_____

_____

_____

Chapter 6
The Dark Cloud of Anxiety, Fear, Stress and Worry

Do not be anxious about anything, but in every situation, by prayer and petition, with thanksgiving, present your requests to God.
Philippians 4:6

Hello, Beautiful!

Today I write to you from the top floor of a hotel. Close your eyes with me and smell the crisp night air. Hear the sounds of Christmas songs along with the voices and laughter of those walking with their loved ones. Gaze upon the strings of soft lights as they twinkle in harmony. Don't you just love this time of year? I do! The buzz of excitement in the air is electric.

My friend Dusti is marrying her love and has invited the hubs and I to celebrate in their union. As I enjoy the lights of the city, my heart is bursting with joy for my friend as she prepares for her big day. What a special moment to share with friends.

Beautiful, I wish I could say I always enjoyed these moments. Regretfully, I realize that fear has gripped me and worry paralyzed, leading me to think of all the *what-if's* as I look down to the street below. Shaking my head, I regret the times in my life when I allowed fear to tie me up in knots. Unfortunately, there have been many moments missed due to a fear of falling- a fear that serves to steal my joy from the simple things in life. I like to think I have it beat, but it still sneaks up on me.

It's time to share a grave challenge we face in our life called anxiety. Anxiety is defined using words such as, "distress," "uneasiness," and "apprehension." It hangs out with its buddies, "fear," "stress," and "worry." Anxiety can create a dark cloud that hangs over you, robbing you of your promised full life.

Remember the beloved character "Pig-Pen" on *Charlie Brown*? He would walk around with a perpetual dust cloud no matter how hard he tried to stay clean. After a moment of immediate dishevelment right after bathing, Pig-Pen would announce to Charlie Brown, *"You know what I am? I'm a dust magnet!"* Pig-Pen came to accept his uncleanliness as being a defining characteristic, and isn't that just like us too? Anxiety grows until it becomes just part of who we are. Some live with anxiety as a disorder their whole lives, going to excessive lengths to avoid a feared object or situation, while allowing it to influence choices and create distress.

⇨**Reflection Time:** Beautiful, can you relate? Can I share that THERE IS HOPE! Please know that reaching out for help does not mean you are giving in to some deep, dark monster! You may very well have believed this lie for most of your life, but seeking help, both mentally and physically, will bring freedom as you learn to face the challenges in your life. Don't be afraid to ask for help, and know that I am praying for you in this very moment!⇦

Do you know how you get nausea in your stomach when you worry over something? Anxiety. Anxiety brings on that overwhelming feeling of panic when you can't breathe as you deliver a presentation. Stress over finishing a project due on

Thursday causes anxiety again. How about when you feel fear standing in line for the roller coaster? Yep! Call it what it is: anxiety. Even thinking about and planning for your future can create an anxious response within you.

My dear friend Shelby can relate to your challenge:

> *"I can be anxious over anything and everything: life, thinking on my future, facing the expectations of others and knowing the life-altering choice of what I want to do with my life at 18 when only three months ago I had to raise my hand to go to the bathroom. These are the things that trigger my anxiety. Goodness, even my anxiety gives me anxiety!"*

Yes, anxiety is quite a challenge. And believe it or not, anxiety does have a purpose. The Anxiety & Behavioral Health Clinic further defines anxiety[3] as, *"A normal, innate emotional alarm response to the anticipation of danger or threat."* They continue by stating that panic is similar to anxiety, *"A normal, innate emotional alarm response to the perception of immediate danger or threat."* God placed inside of us a fight or flight instinct, an instinct designed

---

[3] https://anxietyclinic.fsu.edu/aboutanxiety/main.php

to protect us from harm. For example, you might feel panic when you are facing a rattlesnake and you have to walk around it; or when you smell smoke and have to gather your family and rush out of the house; or even when you must finish that project and need an encouraging boost to finish strong.

Anxiety may have its place; however, we often dwell in it a little too long. Consider the "fight" or "flight" instinct mentioned above, and note that these are active verbs. When anxiety hits, it should move us to take action! But, instead, how often do we choose to dwell in the anxiety, allowing our fear, worry and stress to increase to a point where they affect our health and our decisions. Beautiful, this was never God's plan!

God wants us to *trust in Him with all our hearts and lean not unto our own understanding* (Proverbs 3:5 paraphrased). And He tells us specifically, *"Do not be anxious about anything, but in every situation, by prayer and petition, with*

> Call to Action:
> Trust God and
> lift up your
> requests

thanksgiving, present your requests to God. And the peace of God,

which transcends all understanding, will guard your hearts and your

minds in Christ Jesus" (Philippians 4:6-7).

There is a call to action here: Trust Him and lift up our

requests.

Dear one, God has given us the tools to take back our joy as

we learn to face this dark cloud, which means we must also face

anxiety's buddies: fear, stress and worry. Similar but different,

these joy-killers bring their own rain. But allow me to encourage

you with this truth: **Recognizing your enemy allows you to rebuke**

him with courage and confidence. Don't forget Beautiful, you're

not alone in the storm because your Father is with you! Now let's

face our old enemy fear together!

***

Fear

Fear has paralyzed you at times, hasn't it Beautiful? The

unknown has a tendency to place you in a frozen state, afraid to move. Whereas anxiety is a physical response, fear is defined as, *"An emotion, a feeling brought to light by an impending danger, whether the threat is real or imagined."* And I think it's important to point out that there are two kinds of fear. A second definition describes fear as a *"Reverential awe of our Creator."*[4] You might be thinking, *"What, so should I be afraid of God?"* No, dear girl, when you fear God, your awe creates within you a desire for obedience. Martin Luther said, *"What we, following the scriptures, call the fear of God is not terror or dread, but an awe that holds God in reverence."*[5] This fear, dear one, is a good thing.

But the paralyzing fear expressed in emotion? The apprehension created by this emotion only serves to keep you from marching on. The frozen state you find yourself in, while temporary, can build up until you are too afraid to do anything. We miss many opportunities when we allow our fear to paralyze us, but hear my

---

[4] http://www.dictionary.com/browse/fear?s=t
[5] Described on the basis of Luther's statements by Wilhelm Herrmann

heart: Fear, while it is a paralyzing emotion, can be controlled!

⇨**Reflection Time:** Consider one thing that triggers fear in your life, just one. And I'm not talking about spiders here; I'm referring to the one thing that paralyzes you in your boots. You know what it is, now write it down.⇦

Remember the story of David that I shared with you in a previous letter? David shares with us an intimate moment in Psalm 118:5-7, *"When hard pressed, I cried to the Lord."* David is facing fear with faith. Hard pressed is defined as "squeezed on all sides," which means the only direction David could look was up. And the Lord's answer? *"He brought me into a spacious place."* God would lift David out of his distress, allowing him to see that He was there to help him face his enemy.

He does the same for you, Beautiful, but you too must cry out to the Lord. Pray to Him for help, and allow Him to be your Helper as He thaws with love the ice that paralyzes you.

May I have a moment of transparency here? Fear has been one of my joy-killers. Fear over the possibility of a smoke detector "starting" a fire would raise my anxiety level. Yes, you read correctly. And it wasn't a silly, "hide in my momma's skirts" kind of fear. It was a paralyzing "hide under the covers" kind of fear. It was a "cannot move in the line to the roller coaster" fear. It was a sweating, on the verge of tears, "please don't ask me to move" kind of fear.

I get it, truly I do. But can I share that over the years, God has impressed on me the confidence that He placed in Gideon. I've found great encouragement in the promise found in Joshua 1:9, *"Have I not commanded you? Be strong and courageous. Do not be afraid; do not be discouraged, for the Lord your God will be with you wherever you go."* Wow, **wherever I go?** Yep! God is our Victor. He not only walks with us, but He goes before us, He follows behind us and sometimes He picks us up and carries us. We can be strong because He is strong.

⇨**Reflection Time:** That one thing? Take the piece of paper that you used to write down your fear and write Psalm 118:5-7 next to it. Now repeat after me: "When

'speak fear here' is triggered, I will cry to the Lord, and He will bring me into a spacious place. The Lord is with me; I will not be afraid. What can mere mortals do to me? The Lord is with me; He is my helper. I look in triumph on my enemies!" Now take this piece of paper and place it somewhere visible so that when the fear is triggered, you have it handy to pray. Pray it at the time of your trigger and pray it every day.⇦

***

Stress

Beautiful, there are times when I wish I could take all of the stress in the world away from you. Stress has not been a friend throughout my life, but just as anxiety has a purpose, stress is also part of human design.

The reaction we have to danger is known as the stress response- a natural reaction to help us reach a goal. Studies have demonstrated that as stress increases, performance increases as well. Rene Jein, founder of GoZen.com shares his research that shows positive stress aka "eustress" can be a motivator, increase

focus and energy and also improve both performance and decision

making. However, the flip side is that negative stress can cause

anxiety or concern, decrease performance and lead to mental

and/or physical problems[6].

How do we find the happy medium?

Allow me to introduce you to the prophet Elijah. Elijah had

just experienced two exciting moments of victory, but what

followed was a threat to his life by Queen Jezebel. Elijah did what

any of us might do in a stressful situation; he became afraid and ran

into the wilderness. *"He came to a broom bush (aka juniper tree in*

KJV), sat down under it and prayed that he might die. 'I have had

enough, Lord,' he said, 'I am no better than my ancestors.' Then he

lay down under the bush and fell asleep" (1 Kings 19:4-5a).

⇨**Reflection Time:** How often does the stress in your

life bring you to a place of discouragement, even to the

---

[6] http://www.gozen.com/8-ways-to-help-your-kids-stress-better/

point of wanting to give up? Yes, Elijah ran out of fear, but in the midst of it he cried out to the One whom he knew would help. And Beautiful, God has big shoulders, He can handle your cries of desperation also. ⇦

"All at once an angel touched him and said, 'Get up and eat.' He looked around, and there by his head was some bread baked over hot coals, and a jar of water. He ate and drank and then lay down again" (1 Kings 19:5b-6).

⇨**Reflection Time:** Don't miss this beautiful moment! God directed Elijah to eat. He provided Elijah what was needed physically. Then He blessed him with peace in the process. When we are stressed, it is easy to push emotions down, forget to eat and rest even. But God shows us in Elijah's story how important it is to lean in to self-care. ⇦

"The angel of the Lord came back a second time and touched him and said, 'Get up and eat, for the journey is too much for you.' So he got up and ate and drank. Strengthened by that food,

he traveled forty days and forty nights until he reached Horeb, the mountain of God. There he went into a cave and spent the night." (1 Kings 4:7-9).

⇨**Reflection Time:** Letting go may seem easy, but letting go does not dissipate the dark cloud hanging overhead. I believe Elijah would want us to know that God knows what we need, when we need it and that when stressful situations arise, we can trust Him to provide all we require. Be purposeful in seeking moments of stillness before the Lord. Lean in to the self-care that He designed for you to recover. And in those moments the strength of Christ found in Philippians 4:13 will be yours. ⇦

Elijah regained his physical strength as the Lord appeared to him, asking, *"What are you doing here, Elijah?"* To which he replies, *"I have been very zealous for the Lord God Almighty. The Israelites have rejected your covenant, torn down your altars, and put your prophets to death with the sword. I am the only one left, and now they are trying to kill me too"* (1 Kings 19:9a-10). The Lord responds, *"Go out and stand on the mountain in the presence of the Lord, for the Lord is about to pass by"* (1 Kings 19:11a).

The next part is so good; pay close attention to God's response!

"Then a great and powerful wind tore the mountains apart and shattered the rocks before the Lord, but the Lord was not in the wind. After the wind there was an earthquake, but the Lord was not in the earthquake. After the earthquake came a fire, but the Lord was not in the fire. And after the fire came a gentle whisper" (1 Kings 19:11b-12).

Did you catch it? Let's close our eyes for a moment and pretend we are Elijah. Feel the wind swirling around us, a wind so powerful that it tears the mountains apart. Do you think it would be difficult to stand? As the ground shook, I'm certain we would be looking for something which to grab hold. Then imagine the fire, flames so hot we would struggle to catch our breath. In all these earth-shattering moments, we'd be looking for help, asking *"God, where are you?"* Now close your eyes and breathe for me. Open them and highlight this sentence: *"The Lord was not in the wind, He was not in the earthquake, He was not in the fire."* It's easy to feel sorry for ourselves as we surrender to the earth-shattering moments in life. And easier still to allow our dark cloud to hover, expecting the earth to shake again while hoping for a miracle to take place and sweep us out of the situation. I wonder what Elijah's focus was on in that moment? Remember, Elijah was afraid of being killed. I wonder if God allowed these great feats of nature so that Elijah would recognize His strength, all the while teaching him an important lesson in focus. Would Elijah seek God only when he was faced with the fear of death, or would he stand firm, persevere and be still enough to hear his "gentle whisper" when the chaos subsided?

Call to Action:
Be still and
listen for His
gentle whisper

⇨**Reflection Time:** Beautiful, the wind may be threatening to swirl us off our feet, our foundation may shake and the fire may frighten us with its intensity. But dear one, we will find God and His peace when we learn to be still, pray and listen for

His gentle whisper in these moments of stress. PS- don't forget to highlight the gentle whisper that came after in your Bible.⇦

At the end of this encounter, God reminds Elijah that he is not the only one still standing. In fact, there were 7000 others who chose to follow God in the midst of the evil around them. He then sent Elijah off with great purpose.

Through Elijah's season of stress, God fulfilled His promise to carry out His purpose and fill every need while Elijah modeled prayer and trust. God will carry us, too, into the purpose He has designed. Pray and trust Him to fill all of your needs, Beautiful.

***

Worry

I've saved the best for last. Let's take a walk down dictionary lane, shall we? In anticipation of a situation out of our control, we find ourselves gripped by: "Anxiety" a **physical response**, "fear" an **emotional response**, and "stress" **our response**

to the above. Now let's break down worry. Worry is a persistent thought process of impending doom in a situation. Worry is to the mind what physical pain is to the body ultimately driving anxiety into action. You could say that worry sets the dominoes up for their expected descent.

Worry > Anxiety > Fear > Stress *(Repeat)*

We are not meant to worry. In fact, our Father tells us, *"Look at the birds of the air; they do not sow or reap or store away in barns, and yet your Father feeds them. Are you not much more valuable than they? Can any one of you by worrying add a single hour to your life?"* (Matthew 6:26-27)

So, how do we stop the dominoes from falling? I believe the answer lies in stories and verses of hope in God's love letter. God has given us His Word to write on our hearts. For this very reason, we do not have to fall for the lie of the enemy and sit in the lie of hopelessness he places in our path. Instead, we can courageously face our challenges with confidence that the One who is our Provider, *Jehovah-Jireh* (God our Provider), will give us the strength to overcome. He will provide the courage to rebuke the enemy before the first domino falls. Rick Warren has some great advice to us worriers: *"When you think about a problem over and over in your mind, that's called worry. When you think about God's Word over and over in your mind, that's meditation. If you know how to worry, you already know how to meditate! You just need to switch your attention from your problems to Bible verses."*[7]

Guess what? It's that time again! Time for a call to action, and these verses give us specific instruction. I want you to look up these verses, write them down, and think over them just as Pastor Rick advised. *Let's do this!*

✱✱✱

Trust Him *(Proverbs 3:5-6)*

I know it's difficult to believe in a God we cannot see, but may I ask a couple of questions?

---

[7] http://pastorrick.com/devotional/english/focus-on-scripture-not-worries_530

What do you breathe? *Air.*

Can you see it? *No.*

Guess what, your Father gives air to you in ample supply, even if you can't see it! And if you can trust Him to fill your lungs with life-giving air, why would you not be able to trust Him with the most intimate challenges in your life? God has big shoulders and I promise He can deal with any challenge you throw His way. At the beginning of every day, lay every concern at His feet. You can trust Him to answer your prayer, provide for your need, and be present in your situation.

***

Do not be anxious *(Philippians 4:6a)*

Is it that simple? Can I simply say the words, "Do not be anxious" and be certain that anxiety will not find me?

We don't know what today or tomorrow will bring. In fact, Jesus said, *"Therefore do not worry about **tomorrow**, for **tomorrow** will worry about itself. Each day **has** enough **trouble** of its own"*

(Matthew 6:34). But what we do know with certainty is that we have a Savior who will walk with us through today, tomorrow, and forever.

So if we learned that anxiety is caused by distress, uneasiness and apprehension, with worry being the ugly catalyst to push us down, we have to start there. If you want to fight the anxiety monster, it's time to recognize the things in your life that cause you to worry. You know, the things rooted deep in your heart that cause distress, uneasiness and apprehension. Write them in your journal, let them go and give them to Jesus. Allow Him to go to battle for you as He promised in Exodus 14:14, *"The Lord will fight for you; you need only to be still."*

✳✳✳

Lift up our requests *(Philippians 4:6b)*

Beautiful, I want to take a moment and chat about prayer. I know in your heart that you may believe your prayers are not worthy before a Most High God. But can I tell you that is just not true? Your Heavenly Father wants nothing more than for you to

communicate with Him, to share your dreams, your joys, your fears

and your worries, just as Elijah did under the juniper tree. And can I

tell you a secret? He already knows them. Psalm 44:21b says, *"He*

knows the secrets of the heart."

But if He already knows my need, why do I need to ask?

There's a short story that I think gives us this answer. A

woman sick for twelve years touches the edge of Jesus' cloak. She

says to herself, *"If I only touch His*

cloak, I will be healed" (Matthew

9:21). Jesus turns around and sees

Why does God need me to ask if He already knows?

her, *"Take heart, daughter,"* He said, *"your faith has healed you."*

(Matthew 9:22a). Luke goes a bit deeper in Luke 8 sharing that as

the crowds around Jesus were crushing Him, the woman touched

the edge of his cloak. It is here that Luke highlights the fact that the

woman was not only sick, but **no one** could heal her. (It is

interesting to note that Luke was a doctor, and details were

important). When she touched His cloak, her bleeding stopped as

Jesus asked, *"Who touched me?"*

In Luke's account, we witness three important truths:

- Jesus is always aware of what we need,
- We have a Physician who is never too busy for our need, and
- Faith delights the One who heals our need.

We know this from the words: *"Daughter, your faith has healed you."*

Beautiful, your faith will heal you too. God knows the desires of your heart and is ready to trade your fear for faith, your insecurity for confidence, your worry for calm, your despair for hope, your weakness for strength, and He will trade your anxiety for peace. But free will leads to choice. We have a *choice* to allow Him to share in our life, or else it wouldn't be free will. Just like your very best friend, He is ready and waiting to hear everything- all the good, the bad and the ugly. He wants to heal your heart as He hears your request. So, share it all with your Heavenly Father, dear one, and let Him cover you with *"a peace that surpasses all understanding."*

***

Do not worry *(Matthew 6:26-27)*

Tomorrow has enough trouble of its own, so let it go. You can't add an hour to your life by worrying, so when you lift up your requests to Him, let them go and replace your worry with the things you love.

⇨**Reflection Time:** I know I've given you a lot to consider in this letter, so may I make a suggestion? Write down the things that spoke to you, highlight the topics you would like to consider, and then keep this letter marked so that you can come back to it later. Pray every day over the things you have written, share these things with a trusted friend, and ask God for wisdom in these matters. Our life is a journey- a journey that spans a lifetime. Be encouraged that while you may not take it all in today, a seed has been planted. A seed that I believe God will continue to water and grow throughout your life, so that you may find the healing and peace He has promised.⇦

My friend Shelby has a tip for you:

"When the anxiety cloud is hovering, just listen to soothing music, scribble, journal, or find something to work with your hands to take your mind off of the initial response."

And don't forget to pray.

You've got this, Beautiful, I believe in you! As He holds you in His loving arms in this moment, hear His gentle whisper, *"Daughter, just breathe."* Remember God is with you.

***

I've given you a couple of things to think about in this letter, and I'd like you to add one more thing. Find verses that encourage you in the moments of anxiety, fear, stress and worry, verses such as Philippians 4:6-7. Write them in your journal and pray them when the worry invades. I would also like you to look up words like "strong," "refuge," "fear," "peace," and "hope," and find verses which relate to these words.

There are many resources you can use, but I will share with you these easy ways to find encouragement on specific subjects such as the ones I have shared above.

- If you have a Bible, use the concordance in the back to look up words.
- Download the YouVersion Bible App on your phone and perform a word search.
- A great website to perform a search is BibleGateway.com.
- You can perform a topical search on the website OpenBible.info.
- And if you are having trouble finding verses to encourage you, contact me at www.adaughtersjourney.net. I would love to help you find the encouragement that God has for you in His love story!

God has gifted us with tools to help us in the moment, so know that you can trust Him, beautiful lady!

Love you!

Will write to you soon!

Eve

Things to Remember:

_____

_____

_____

_____

_____

_____

_____

_____

_____

_____

_____

_____

_____

Chapter 7
Finding the Light in the Darkness

The Word gave life to everything that was created, and his life brought light to everyone. The light shines in the darkness, and the darkness can never extinguish it.
John 1:4-5

Hello, Beautiful!

Yes, it's Monday, and before you say *"Ugh, I hate Mondays,"* I have a challenge for you.

I am fascinated with the reaction of others when I smile at them. Some smile graciously in return, while others avert their eyes quickly, and still others frown as if to say, "What's wrong with her?" Oh, if only we knew how our facial expressions reflect the state of our hearts! My fascination has led to a challenge. I'm calling it #findthelight.

Will you join me in my challenge? Yes, even on Monday!

***

I believe there is a great light that shines within all of us. In fact, John 1 even tells us this is true: *"His life brought light to everyone."* This light shines bright when we are born. And the truth is that life experiences can sustain our light or cause it to dim. And I'm going to bring that word "choice" back into our conversation- we can **choose** to allow our light to shine outward to the world, we can hide the light from others, or we can allow our light to be extinguished as our life spirals out of control.

I would like to share these different reactions with you today, and here's a heads up: it will seem heavy, but it's necessary, so bear with me.

Up to this point we've explored practical tips to help in the moments when you feel unloved, sad, afraid, worried, anxious and stressed. I hope these encourage you and serve as light in the darkness, but I know that sometimes the darkness can seem overwhelming, so much so that you feel as if you're in a dark hole without a ladder. My heart cries out for you, for your feelings of exhaustion, the suffocating stillness wrapping you in a cocoon of depression, and the culmination of self-hate, even self-injury. The light can seem so far away that you question its existence, but today, my dear, I am lighting a candle for you and sending it through these pages to remind that the light within you is still there. Remember: *"...the darkness can **never** extinguish it."*

There may come a time in your life when the darkness feels like a blanket, leaving no room for the light. Beautiful, I wish I could shield you from this, but I can't. All I can do is share the

> You never know whose light you can rekindle by shining your own.

hope that carried me through my own journey. And in an effort to help others who are stumbling through life; I hope to shine light in the heart that perhaps is holding onto darkness. You may never experience this personally: oh, I thank our God in Heaven for this blessing if this is the case. But please be aware and prepared for others who will. As physician and Nobel Peace Prize winner Albert

Schweitzer said, *"At times our light goes out and is rekindled by a spark from another person. Each of us has cause to think with deep gratitude of those who have lighted the flame within us."* [8] **You never know whose light you can rekindle by shining your own, but this will require you to recognize the signs.**

Let's explore the deep issues of depression, self-hate and self-injury. I too have faced my own challenges in the darkness and with the help of *El Roy,* the God who sees, I'm finding the courage every day to live in His light and be a reflection to others who have yet to face their own challenges.

* * *

Depression

I had a dream one night that I was walking along a wet and soggy path when all of a sudden the ground beneath me gave way. Surrounded by soft earth and creepy crawlies, I found myself six feet under, rocks cutting into my skin, and tree roots burrowing all

---

[8] https://www.brainyquote.com/quotes/albert_schweitzer_402282

around me. The cocoon created by the soft packed earth felt warm and safe yet terrifyingly cold at the same time. I awoke shaking with the light of a revelation: this is how my depression felt! In my cocoon of loneliness and despair, I found it easy to allow the darkness to settle in and convince me of the lie that I was completely alone with nobody to care about my life. I felt warm and safe, but the truth is that I was slowly allowing the challenges of life to push me into the abyss, unaware of the effect they were having on my emotions, my family, my relationships and my life. I was oblivious to the truth that **there was a way out**.

Looking back on that season of life, I remember the verse that says: *"The grace of our Lord was poured out on me abundantly, along with the faith and love that are in Christ Jesus"* (1 Timothy 1:14). Oh, the grace upon grace upon grace! While I was six feet under, my Savior was digging a trench around me. He was fortifying the well of my sorrow, and in a moment I will never forget, I would look up. Can you imagine my plight for a few moments? Paralyzed, with no possible escape in sight, you open your eyes and see the

Light, so small at first, only to grow larger and brighter as the earth falls away from your body. And then you see it: His beautiful, outstretched hand, magnificent and scarred. With tears in your eyes, you look into His own as you ask, *"Why would you rescue someone like me, ready to give up, desperate for love, a nobody, why?"* And in an unforgettable moment, blinded by the love in His eyes you hear, *"Because I love you so much. Now take my outstretched arm, my love endures forever"* (Psalm 136:12).

⇨**Reflection Time:** Dear one, know that I am praying for you. I pray that in the moment you feel the cold depths of depression wrap dark hands around you, you too will look up and see the small light as it brightens through the beautiful love within His eyes as you glimpse the grace upon grace that He has for you. It was this moment that healed my desperate heart wrapped in the cold darkness of depression. I believe that His light will heal your heart also.⇦

***

Self-hate

I was six years old, with glasses, a gawky gait, brown wavy hair and a smile that wouldn't quit. Big teeth, big brown eyes, and louder than an old woman with a broken hearing aid. I laugh when I think about the naive questions I asked. I smile when I think about my persevering spirit in seeking answers. I cry when I think about those who didn't encourage this beautiful, energetic and creative soul toward this truth, *"The only stupid question is the one you never ask."* When I look back, I think this is the season when I began to question my voice, and I recognize that my insecurities began to rise as I asked the questions, *"Am I stupid? Why am I unlovable?"*

So many things I could say to that beautiful, insecure little girl, and honestly I think that little girl is in all of us.

Let's not forget the girl on your social media feed discussed in a previous letter. She has so many of the same insecurities that we do, and the advice from my friend Emma bears repeating:

"We must avoid contemplating our self-worth and calculating what others see in us, instead we should recognize who God says we are, and in this we find our true colors."

⇨**Reflection Time:** I believe this lesson is for all of us. If you haven't quite grasped this truth and live with hatred toward yourself for the things that you are or aren't, it's never too late. **Don't allow the enemy's lies to tear you down; instead allow the Creator's truth to build you up**! Please Beautiful, if you must, re-read my letters about who loves you, who defines you and how beautiful He thinks you are, because in God's Word **you will begin to see the Light that shines within as your reflection is revealed through the Father's eyes.** ⇦

I promised you it would get heavy, didn't I? Do we need a break from the heaviness for a moment? I have a sweet story for you. Every day when I leave work,

> See your reflection through The Father's Eyes

I spend thirty minutes driving home. As I walk in the door, my sweet basset hound, Max, greets me with a duck in his mouth. No, not a real one, but our fair-feathered, stuffed friend is quite the quacker! (*Say that three times fast!*) Max is so cute when he sees me come in the door, excited as he shows me the beloved prize he is presenting. Tail wagging, he teases me with his present and runs to the kitchen expecting the chase to ensue. The chase will continue for about five minutes until finally he drops the prize and awaits his reward, a full hug with a back rub (*for him, not me*). As I lean down and place my arms around him, he places his head into the crook of my neck. You see, he doesn't want just a pat on the head, he wants a full hug that is close enough to hear the beat of my heart.

My dog is giving me a gift, not the duck, but the hug. Every night, as I sit in this moment of love, I consider the love of our Father as He stands outside of space and time, meeting us right where we are. He is always ready to give us just what we need. When we run to our Abba Father, He pulls us close so we can hear the beat of His heart. And within the safety of His loving arms, His still small whisper encourages us to go on.

Unfortunately, it's easy to get lost in our struggles, and we miss Him standing right in front of us. If I came home and dismissed my fur-baby Max, I would miss out on an extravagant gift. But how many gifts do we miss when we dismiss our Father?

How much do we miss when we hate ourselves, even to the point of injury?

***

Self-Injury

We're going to go a little uphill now, so expect some level of difficulty. We've come to the topic of self-injury, and I have to admit this is a tough subject for me. I feel; however, that we need to shed light on this subject.

What is self-injury? Web-MD describes it:

Self-injury, also called self-harm, self-mutilation, or simply cutting, is defined as any intentional injury to one's own body. Usually, self-injury leaves marks or causes tissue damage. Self-injury can involve any of the following behaviors: Cutting, burning (or "branding" with hot objects), excessive body piercing or tattooing, picking at skin or reopening wounds, hair-pulling, head-banging, hitting (with hammer or other object), bone-breaking. Self-injury usually occurs when people face what seem like overwhelming or distressing feelings. It can also be an act of rebellion or rejection of parents' values and a way of individualizing oneself. Most who engage in self-injury act alone rather than in groups. They also attempt to hide their behavior.[9]

Web-MD continues by stating that:

"Self-injury occurs more often among adolescent females. It's often seen in people with a history of physical, emotional, or sexual abuse, obsessive-compulsive disorder or eating disorders. Individuals raised in families that discouraged expression of anger can also participate in self-injury. And often individuals who lack skills to express their emotions and lack a good social support network find themselves engaging in self-injury."

I'm not attempting to define anyone clinically, but my heart hurts over the gut-splitting, heart-wrenching stories of sadness leading to the point of injuring one's own body. I grieve over some of the things I've heard. The great despair that leads a person to

---

[9] https://www.webmd.com/anxiety-panic/guide/self-injuring-hurting#1

this point would bring even a strong man to his knees. In fact, I'll bet you have a friend who is struggling with self-injury even now. More reason for us to have this hard conversation so we can begin to understand it for them and for us. And if you're one who needs help, remember the words in my last letter, ***"By reaching out for help, you are not giving into some deep dark monster. I know you've believed this for most of your life. Seeking help, both physically and mentally, will bring freedom in the end as you learn to face the challenges in your life."*** Please ask for help, and know that I am praying for you in this very moment!"

This encouragement applies if you're depressed, anxious, worried, afraid, stressed, if you struggle with self-hate and even if you are considering, or are participating in some form of self-injury. It's never too late to find hope, Beautiful.

This topic is deep, so I have decided to bring in some friends. Allow them to encourage your heart as they have encouraged mine.

We'll start with my dear friend Rosemarie, a sophomore in

college. Her mission in life is to encourage other young women with

the knowledge that they are empowered to find the love and peace

of our Father in their struggle. She's an avid advocate of the non-

profit *"To Write Love on Her Arms"* TWLOHA[10], and she shares a bit

about it below.

Rosemarie says:

*"Self-injury is triggered in many ways; there is so much pent-up emotion that you get lost thinking, "It's inside of me, so it must be towards me." Find a way to express your emotion and deal with it: Working with your hands, writing, drawing-- even on yourself-- these are all ways that you can divert the emotion in the moment. My pastor once recommended giving yourself a 5-10 second window. If you react within that window of 10 seconds, you **will** react negatively, but if you wait to react until the window is over, the response will be much different.*

I highly recommend you read the book by the name of: "If You Feel Too Much" by Jamie Tworkowski. Jamie is the founder of "To Write Love on Her Arms," or TWLOHA, a non-profit movement dedicated to presenting hope and finding help for people struggling with depression, addiction, self-injury and suicide. In this book, he shares stories of his life where he found himself dealing with great emotion, and he uses his stories to encourage us by saying, 'It's okay, me too.'"

---

[10] https://twloha.com/

Wow, me too! Can you say this?

Do me a favor, take your right hand and place it on your left shoulder, take your left hand and place it on your right shoulder, now squeeze! Beautiful, consider this a virtual hug from me to you!!

A Call to Action: Go check out TWLOHA and find hope!

Remember Emma? She has some encouragement on the subject:

> *"Sometimes people tell you that it will get better, but if you don't see it on the horizon you begin to believe "better" doesn't exist, so you consider taking matters into your hands. But please hear me, it does exist! Faith is believing in the unseen. Hold on to this, my friend, and have faith that things will get better."*

Faith is believing in the unseen, dear one. Just as air sustains life, **God has your back, and if you lose faith, well, feel free to borrow some of mine.**

Now for my friend Shelby, remember her? She was the one who encouraged you through anxiety.

Shelby says:

> *"I struggled with self-harm. I blamed myself for the*

struggles of my friends, thinking that if they hurt themselves, then I needed to hurt myself as well.

My triggers included fighting with my parents, anxiety attacks and the honest truth that sometimes I just wanted to do it. As with any addiction, you have this "want" to do it. Sometimes I would just be sitting in my room, wrapped up in the darkness finding myself dependent on the action itself. After a time, I realized I didn't know how to do anything else. It became an escape from all other emotions.

Then one day I was inspired by my favorite singer, Britt Nicole, who showed me God and His love. Through the songs, "When She Cries" and "All This Time," I realized I wanted more than what I was consuming in my life. Her music was real, relatable, and helped me realize I didn't want to be defined by self-harm.

How did I stop? I made a conscious decision that I didn't want to be defined by my struggle; it wasn't worth it for me to go down that road. True, it may seem like it was a quick fix, but my self-harm was only creating more problems and anxiety than it ever helped. So, when I wanted to harm myself, I would use a red pen and draw lines on myself. I would write, sing music, and color. I learned that by delving into these habits, it would take my mind off of the trigger."

While I couldn't relate with Shelby's specific life experiences, I could relate to the underlying emotions, and my heart hurt for the little girl inside who was straining to find the light in the darkness.

I truly hope that Shelby's encouragement helps as you face your struggles. I hope that she has inspired you to see the light God is shining on you.

May we recognize this as an opportunity to help others.

**

Love those who are struggling

Now let's change gears and place our focus on the struggles of others. At some point in your life, you may have a friend who is struggling with these heavy topics, and you may not fully understand what they are going through. If this is you, some friends of mine have some encouragement for you as well:

Rosemarie continues:

*"**W**hen you are the "friend," it's a lot of hard love and lots and lots of listening. At the beginning, celebrate often: "Oh my goodness, we made it 6 hours, YAY!!!" Recognize the achievements remembering that everything is sensitive, fresh, and no rebuking! If they fall back, say "I'm sorry for your struggle, but hey look, we made it a full day!" Be genuinely excited and love them through the process. It's not easy, but genuine care and love will help them to see the light on the other side. And please, don't be discouraged if they fall, just pray for them and continue to be there in their time of need. As they are further along in their recovery and begin to separate from their self-injury, only then can you speak more truth in love to them. But remember, even in the*

rebuke, celebrate often!"

I love this! **Celebrate often!** Isn't that what friendship is all about, celebrating the good times and encouraging in the bad?

My friend Katelyn has a great suggestion for a friend who is struggling:

> *"When your friend is struggling, ask them to open their hands and close their eyes. Tell them to picture all of the pain, struggle, stress, and anything that weighs them down, as a ball in their hand. Curl their fingers up as if they are holding the ball and ask them "Do you feel it?" Then instruct them to overturn their hands letting all of these things fall from their fingers visualizing their burdens falling at the foot of the Cross. Remind them that God's love will be all that remains."*

I love this idea of visual release! We recognize that the power Jesus gave is ours! His sacrifice on the Cross took our sin, our pain, our struggle and our stress as his blood covered each one. In their place we have His great love, which will always cover the things that threaten to grab hold of us.

I realize my letter has stretched long, but I do hope and pray it has helped you. There is one more thing I'd like to share with you, and then we will get to the challenge.

Through every struggle you ever face, you have a choice to give up, give in, or persevere through, and in my next letter I'll share practical tips to help you persevere when you face a challenge. In the meantime, soak in the verse I shared at the beginning of my letter: "*The Word gave life to everything created, and his life brought light to everyone. The light shines in the darkness, and the darkness can never extinguish it* (John 1:4-5 NIV).

***

A Call to Action: I would like you to write down the verse above in your journal along with this Jewish Hanukkah Prayer:

All the darkness of the world cannot extinguish the light of a

single candle,

yet one candle can illuminate all the darkness.

- Jewish Hanukkah Prayer

Oh, and let's not forget our challenge! At the beginning of my letter, I shared a movement called #findtheLight. If the Word gave life to everything created, then that means that we can find Light in everything created, right?

My challenge to you, *#findtheLight*. Every day, find one person that you look straight in the eye and smile. Then search for one blessing that brings light to this dark world and thank God for this gift. Feel free to share on social media using the hashtag: *#findthelight.* Write it down, share it with your friends, and pass it forward. Oh, and I would love to hear your stories at https://youthroughthefatherseyes.com/.

May we all shine our light in this dark world!

Love you, Beautiful! Til our next letter,

Eve

Things to Remember:

_____

_____

_____

_____

_____

_____

_____

_____

_____

_____

_____

_____

_____

Chapter 8
Challenges and Blessings

Consider it pure joy, my brothers and sisters, whenever you face trials of many kinds, because you know that the testing of your faith produces perseverance. Let perseverance finish its work so that you may be mature and complete, not lacking anything.
James 1:2-4

Merry Christmas, Beautiful!

Today is Christmas, and I am so excited to write to you!

This is a perfect day to share two topics near and dear to my heart: challenges and blessings, both of which, I've experienced in the last 24 hours, revealing much over the course of my journey about who God is and who I am.

As I sit here considering the ups and downs of life, I must admit it hasn't been a bed of roses, and to be honest, I wouldn't have it any other way. At 16 years old, I knew what it was like to experience great love and heartbreak, I recognized what it was to pass and fail, and every day I met challenges and blessings that

prepared me for this season of

life. **Beautiful, I'm here to help**

you to see your challenges for

what they are, faith builders.

> Challenges are
> Faith Builders.

***

Singing was everything to me, and from the time I was

three years old, music seemed to flow from my heart and lips in

wild abandon. Sometimes I would hum a quiet tune, and others I

would belt at the top of my lungs. Music is part of my DNA, but I

must admit I had a problem in my early years of musical maturity.

Insecurity, one of my greatest challenges in life, held me back. I so

wanted to play the piano, the guitar and to write music, but the

challenge of insecurity created a chasm in my identity, making me

question my purpose. A nasty little bugger, insecurity stole my joy

as I bought the lies it told me. It's easy to forget truth in the midst

of these thoughts: *"The mountain is too high to climb, or the task too scary to accomplish."* Or how about *"I'm not good enough to succeed at this challenge."* I began to wonder if the insecure voice in my head knew my limits better than I did.

Have you ever had a season such as this? I wonder:

What if we're missing a critical part of the process when we believe the lie?

Unfortunately, I listened to this voice and allowed it to redefine me for a time, even to the point of temporarily letting go of the dream I once had. However, let me tell you, that wasn't the end of my story. The *Alpha* and *Omega* (the beginning and the end) had a different plan, and His purpose is still in action.

I remember the anxiety I felt over my last try out for All-State Chorus. Although I had previously attended, my anxiety and fear were so great that I quit. It was one of those moments when I needed to be encouraged with the truth that I would face challenges in my journey, but I didn't have to let a challenge beat me down. Allow my experience to encourage you: the fear of failure may be strong, but please don't forget this truth, ***the only true*** *failure is when you fail to try.*

⇨**Reflection Time:** What is your challenge, Beautiful? We all have them and it is time to face yours. Write it in your journal and then write down this truth, *I can do all things through Christ who strengthens me* (Philippians 4:13 paraphrased).⇦

Challenges have a way of sneaking up on you when least expected. Often your defenses are down, but can I share a secret with you? Regardless of how a challenge comes to you, **preparing ahead of time not only prepares you for your current challenge, but also for those to come.**

Jada shares with us:

"One of my major challenges has been facing rejection."

So how do we plan for a challenge? How do you plan for the rejection letter? We've discussed the importance of preparing for those things that create hardship in our life. The truth is that we can and must prepare for any challenge. Not to say that we know about the challenge before it happens, but we can prepare by recognizing our weaknesses and speaking truth in the face of our challenge. How does Jada recommend preparing for rejection? First, recognize that a rejection letter isn't a death warrant, but is only a door closing. Second, realize that God has another plan with an open door to something greater.

⇨**Reflection Time:** I've shared some of my weaknesses, but do you know yours? If you know your weaknesses, you are better equipped to persevere through them, recognizing that it is not necessarily your strength that pushes you through the challenge, but His.⇦

Dictionary.com defines a challenge as, *"Something that by its nature or character serves as a call to battle, contest, special effort, etc."* It further defines challenge as, *"Difficulty in a job or undertaking that is stimulating to one engaged in it."*[11] If a challenge requires special effort, then we must train ourselves to

---

[11] http://www.dictionary.com/browse/challenge?s=t

push through the pain. If a challenge results in difficulty, then we must train our minds to push through the difficulty. If a challenge results in a closed door, then we must train our hearts to wait for the next open door. But did you catch the bonus point in the second definition? Challenges requiring effort are stimulating. Our brain wants to be challenged, our muscles need to be challenged, and the truth is our lives yearn to be challenged; this is all part of the process. Jada encourages us with this:

> "*A rejection letter challenges us to depend on God and to trust Him for the next open door as we watch a door close.*"

We begin to learn it is through the challenge that we grow, mature, and recognize that dependence on our Heavenly Father is necessary to help us through all of life. Dependence on God is so much greater than a lonely life of independence and it's where we find our true strength.

When you are weak, He is strong.

After we recognize our weaknesses and accept that we can depend on a God who is in control, we must learn to change the way we think. Our thoughts are powerful, guiding us into action or inaction, and when we take captive our thoughts, we recognize we have the power to control the emotions that can lead to our greatest challenges.

How does this work?

***

Guard your heart

"Above all else, guard your heart, for everything you do flows from it" (Proverbs 4:23). With free will, we have the freedom to allow anything into our mind. But is it prudent to invite in anything? God wants us to have a full life. To do so means we must guard our heart from the things that steal life, such as activities that create depressing thoughts, or words that weigh us down and hurt our hearts. And yes we must guard our hearts from fear leading us to inaction.

⇨**Reflection Time:** This is a BIG DEAL Beautiful! Take a moment to inventory the things in your life that create these heavy and depressing thoughts. Some examples may include: social media, television shows, excessive screen time or school. Perhaps even a relationship creates a spiral of depressing thoughts in your mind. Write these down for me, we will come back to them later. ⇦

***

What should I think about?

Great question, Beautiful! Philippians 4:8 says, *"Finally, brothers and sisters, whatever is true, whatever is noble, whatever is right, whatever is pure, whatever is lovely, whatever is admirable - if anything is excellent or praiseworthy - **think** about such **things**."* You may not be in control of your circumstances, but you are in control of your thoughts. Beautiful, the POWER is yours, so claim it!

***

Speak truth to your Challenge

Just as you have the power to take control of your thoughts, you also have the power to speak God's truth in the face of your challenge. For example: you're frustrated over a pending test you are studying for on a topic that you just don't understand. You have two choices in this moment:

1-   You can give up and accept a bad grade.

OR

2-   You can speak truth to your challenge and claim a good grade by saying, *"God said I can do all things through Christ who strengthens me."* You can pray, *"Lord, I'm having trouble learning this topic, please grant me wisdom and focus to understand and do well on this test."* Moving forward is a step of faith trusting that He will fulfill His promise. Be prepared to God to answer according to His will. Whether He inspires you to work harder or places someone in your midst to help, remember, just like the diamond we learned about in Chapter 4, the process is all part of the journey.

⇨**Reflection Time:** Let's look at your list of negative thought generators again. Is there anything on this list that you can give up? Consider a fast from social media for a week, or perhaps replace the television show with a good book or worship music. How about putting the device down and taking a walk? Give up your worry and replace it with God's truth about who He says you are and what you can do. (Go back and read Philippians 4:13 again!) And if a relationship is causing you to spiral into depressive thoughts, consider talking to a trusted adult who can help you navigate next steps to guard your heart. You do not have to be a hostage to negative thoughts, dear one. Remember, when you know Jesus, you have the power of Christ within you! I will say it again, CLAIM IT! ⇦

Beautiful, if you change the way you think, you will change the way you feel. In God's Word, He shares the formula for changing the way you think. We have only scratched the surface. Ask Him to show you, then read and apply His Word to your circumstance, and you will find that not only can you face your mountain, but also find little blessings in the process. ***Abba Father***

delights in those who believe!

I think this is a great transition into blessings; what do you think? We like to think that blessings are the opposite of challenges, but challenges can *lead* us into recognizing our true blessings.

Jada gives us an example:

"Comparison, coined "the thief of all joy," makes you feel less than. You're so busy comparing SAT scores, who is going to prom with whom, and what college everyone is going to that you forget to enjoy the now, ultimately missing out on so much.

But the truth is, in my Junior and Senior years when comparison was strong, we had so many activities planned just for us. I had to learn to be grateful for God's blessings in the community of people where God had placed me. In thankfulness, God gave me a greater awareness of all His blessings.

You soon realize to be grateful for what you have; the little things become big things when they are gone."

We become more aware, humble and grateful when we recognize our Father walking alongside us. I find that it is in this knowledge that we see blessings everywhere. Jada mentions gaining a "greater awareness of all blessings." Oh, the joy that follows when we become more aware of God's blessings! We will call them "God's fingerprints." The more grateful you are, the more grateful you become, and inevitably the more you'll see His fingerprints everywhere!

I could give you a laundry list of blessings I have witnessed over the years, but today, I will share three circumstances that had God's fingerprints interwoven throughout. Please understand we don't all see blessings in the same manner, but to be aware of their existence helps us hunt for them.

***

Blessing #1 - My Heavenly Father

There was a time when I didn't believe, a time I was ready to walk away from my faith, my Heavenly Father and everything I thought I believed. I didn't realize the grief that followed was a direct consequence of this action. Remember the story I told in an earlier letter of being in a cold, dark hole? I was lost and seemingly alone in my depression, and I truly felt as if there was no way out.

The walls of my cold, dark place threatened to rob me of every breath. When I saw the loving hand of my Father as He knelt down to pull me out, I turned back to Him. And when I did, the beauty of His reconciliation was a blessing unlike any other. I am still brought to tears when I read the story in Luke 15 and recognize the reflection of my story in that of the prodigal son.

Blessing #2 - My Family

My family has been an incredible blessing to me! When I meet a challenge in life, there is always a family member to help me through. We may not always see eye-to-eye, but the love of family has allowed me to witness the unconditional love of the Father. I remember on my 16th birthday when I was going through an extremely difficult time, my dad invited me to dinner. As the oldest of five girls, being invited to dinner by your dad was more than a treat; it was a miracle! It was a moment I would never forget because I felt so special and loved.

⇨**Reflection Time:** Beautiful, this is my personal blessing that I share with you. Many do not have family members that encourage and empower them. If this is your story, seek out those in your life who do. They may not be blood related, but they are family just the same. ⇦

Blessing #3 - Serving

I'll share more on this blessing in my next letter, but serving has been a beautiful blessing that continuously gives back. There are so many stories I could tell, but I'll share one. Several years ago a young woman came through our high school ministry. She was only there for about nine months, but in those nine months I watched her faith grow by leaps and bounds! Her growth began as she asked questions, many questions I often didn't have answers for. But boy, was she was on fire! And over the course of time, her seeking and searching through God's Word drew her closer to Him. When it came time for her to leave, she was anxious about going home, worried she would lose what she had gained. But within three months she not only found a local church to attend, but joined the worship team! I'll never forget this season when I caught a glimpse of God's glory as He moved in her life. It reminded me how Moses experienced a glimpse of the glory of God in Exodus 33:22-23. Watching God's fingerprints move keeps me going on those days when I don't always see the blessing in the task.

⇨**Reflection Time:** What blessings can you recall? Just start with one and praise your Father in Heaven for this gift in your life. I promise you they are there, but you may have to open your eyes to see them.⇦

I find it interesting that some blessings I encounter begin with a challenge. I wonder, is a lesson to be found here? **Perhaps the true blessing we find in the challenge is the persevering spirit that encourages us to never quit.**

This leads me to one last blessing I would like to share with you. At the beginning of my letter, I shared with the challenge of insecurity that pushed me to quit a dream of singing. Well I have a little secret to share. About nine years ago I thought I had lost all ability to sing. In fact, at the time, I considered myself punished for walking away from what I thought was God's purpose in my life. Then miraculously, four years ago, God gave me the most amazing gift; He blessed me with the ability to write: poetry, song lyrics and now this my second book, all gifts from our Heavenly Father who restored me back to Him and rebirthed the dream I thought I lost.

Oh, and slowly I am regaining the voice I once had, exciting right? Insight into the heart of God and the great love He has for me has been the true blessing through this and every challenge to follow.

> For every season there is a reason; seek to find the reason and you will find joy in the season.

Beautiful, remember He is the Alpha and Omega. He has the first and the last word dear one, so allow Him to work your challenge into the blessing He designed as you remember this:

For every season there is a reason; seek to find the reason and you will find joy in the season.

***

A Call to Action:

First- Journal about a challenge you are struggling with and include the call to action listed under challenges earlier in my letter. Over the next week, prayerfully apply these actions to your challenge and watch God move!

Second- Remember the list of negative thought generators you wrote down? Commit to an action plan to replace those things with positive thought generators. Pray for God to help you stay committed. Consider an accountability partner to remind you of God's truth when you are tempted toward the negative.

Third- Seek to find one new blessing and journal your findings daily. Consider it your "Blessing Scavenger Hunt." God's fingerprints are everywhere and if there is one thing I know, when you begin to recognize them, He delights in helping you connect the dots! Oh and don't forget to share a prayer of thanks to your Heavenly Father for His provision of challenges and blessings!

Love you, Beautiful,

Till next time,

Eve

Things to Remember:

_____

_____

_____

_____

_____

_____

_____

_____

_____

_____

_____

_____

_____

_____

_____

Chapter 9
A Servant Heart is a Grateful Heart

Above all, love each other deeply, because love covers over a multitude of sins. Offer hospitality to one another without grumbling. Each of you should use whatever gift you have received to serve others, as faithful stewards of God's grace in its various forms.
1 Peter 4:8-10

Hello Beautiful!

The Christmas season is winding down, and the community

is finding its way back into routine. My heart has always had a

special place for the season when we celebrate the birth of our

Hero *Yeshua* (Jesus, our Rescuer, our Deliverer). I love the joy on

young faces as they revive us with awe and wonder, the hope in

those who find the greatest gift of all in salvation, and the beauty of

love experienced as a servant heart connects one to another. **We**

experience a heart awakening when we slow down and focus on

the Reason for the season. Do you know that feeling? Christmas shines a light on the greatest commandments Jesus gave: to *"Love the Lord your God with all your heart and with all your soul and with all your mind. This is the first and greatest commandment. And the second is like it: Love your neighbor as yourself"* (Matthew 22:37-38).

I expect you may question if you have the time or energy to serve another person, but I've seen that when I love and genuinely serve another, the time and energy seem to regenerate. Consider a conduit of electricity: the conduit serves as a pathway for the electricity to travel from the source (an electrical power supply) to the endpoint (a light bulb). When you serve, you become the wiring, the source is God, the power flowing through is The Holy Spirit, and the endpoint is the person you have the opportunity to serve. Through this current of love you are charged and recharged by the love the Father transfers through you to the one you serve! If only we could truly understand this, we would be recharged, continuously, all year long and not only during the season of

Christmas.

This letter to you, just like Christmas, is going to be special. While there is so much I could share on the topic of serving, I think the stories shared by those with boots on the ground would give you much greater insight to the beauty of this gift. After they share, I will wrap things up, okay?

Read Lisa's beautiful story:

> "*On Christmas day, we visited the homeless in tent cities, giving soup, clothes and prayer. I'd told the Lord if it was just one we came to minister to, that would be ok. Well, after the fourth place we went, there she was- a scared young woman who found herself homeless after one mistake. She was sent to jail and lost her child, her job and car. She received Jesus with tears flowing. My friend gave her a number to get off the streets. That girl alone made it worth going on Christmas Day.*"

Charles would like to share:

> "*Many years ago I interviewed for a job working with children and families at a Christian agency. After the interview this administrator touched me on the shoulder and smiled a knowing smile, asking, "Do you have a servant spirit?" I paused and responded, "I think I do. What do you mean?" His eyes filled with love, and he pointed to the waiting room where a woman sat quietly. He asked that I just watch for a moment. The woman was well into her*

seventies and wore a printed cotton dress that appeared like her, comfortable and well worn. Her soft wrinkled face wore a slight smile and as each child came through the door, they came to her for a moment and held on to the side of the dress, leaning close. She gave each one a smile and a hug. While their parents took care of their business each child waved to her as she smiled and waved to them. An hour passed as I was waiting for a tour of the facility. At least a dozen children sat at her side and received this attention. After my tour, I asked who the woman was. The reply I received was, 'One of God's servants.'

Before today neither she nor the children had ever met. She loved those children before she ever met them. Charles Wright told me that almost forty years ago. To this day I remember Cora May Thompson, or Mom Thompson as she was lovingly called, the woman who encouraged me to see all people through those eyes. I love you Cora May, like you loved those children, unconditionally."

Jenna has a sweet story:

"*I* am a student at Georgia State where in the middle of campus is Woodruff Park. During a rough patch in July, I was walking to class through the park around 9 am and a homeless man walked up to me and said "Ma'am, I wanted to let you know that God loves you, and you matter." Afraid for a brief moment, I prayed, "God, tell me what to do." In a flash my perspective changed, and I realized someone who didn't have a roof over his head, who didn't know where his next meal was coming from, was speaking truth into me. I had whiplash, and I knew I had to give him my food. And what did he do? With a smile he humbly rejected my gift for himself. What he didn't know was I had extra. After asking again, he proceeded to take my gift and offer it to others.

You must understand, I haven't seen the man since, but I know he was a blessing sent from God to serve me in that moment."

In each story, I hope you've recognized a common theme.

Each person who served was:

- Willing,

- Connected to the source,

- Endowed with what are called spiritual gifts used to

  transmit the love the Father poured through them.

What are spiritual gifts? Well, I'm glad you asked.

Remember my letter about purpose? I shared one of my favorite

verses by the Apostle Paul, *I can do all things through Christ who*

strengthens me (Philippians 4:13 paraphrased).

In the New Testament, we find another letter Paul wrote to

the church of Corinth, 1 Corinthians, a beautiful letter with a

treasure toward the end in chapters 12 and 13.

As children of God, we have a Helper, The Holy Spirit. *(Do*

you remember Him, introduced in my second letter as God in Spirit

form?) Paul explains that the Holy Spirit distributes different kinds of gifts, different kinds of service and different kinds of working" (1 Corinthians 12:4-6 paraphrased). Paul goes on to share examples of these gifts: wisdom, knowledge (teaching), faith, healing, miracles, prophecy, discernment, speaking in different languages (tongues) and interpretation of different languages (tongues). In Romans 12:6-8, Paul lists these additional gifts: serving or ministering, encouragement (exhortation), giving, leadership and showing mercy. In Ephesians 4:11, Paul places names on specific callings resulting from spiritual gifts such as: apostles, prophets, evangelists, pastors and teachers.

In 1 Corinthians 12, Paul goes on to explain how the body of the Church is one with Christ at the Head, each part of the body needing the other: *"If one part suffers, every part suffers with it; if one part is honored, every part rejoices with it"* (1 Corinthians 12:26). Paul closes this chapter explaining that with all of these gifts, if we do not have love, we just make a lot of noise.

Chapter 13 defines love this way: patient, kind, it does not envy, it does not boast, it is not proud, it does not dishonor others, it is not self-seeking, it is not easily angered, it keeps no record of wrongs, it does not delight in evil but rejoices with the truth, it always protects, trusts, hopes, it always perseveres, **love never fails** (1 Corinthians 13:4-8a paraphrased).

⇨**Reflection Time:** Take a moment Beautiful, and think of all the people who add value to your life. Consider how they have encouraged, loved and blessed you with their spiritual gifts. See how God uses spiritual gifts to pour his love into his creation?⇦

I adore these companion chapters from 1 Corinthians. Like two bookends, chapter 12 is the toolbox, listing all the tools we have access to, whereas chapter 13 is the instruction manual for using these tools. It's as if Paul is instructing us how to carry out the commandments Jesus gave: *love God and love your neighbor.* ***Notice the emphasis on love?***

It's not rocket science. God has given us the tools, and He uses us to deliver love to those in our path. We only need a willing heart, and that, my dear, is where you come in! There are some pretty amazing stories above, and I hope you have enjoyed them. Now it's your turn:

⇨**Reflection Time:** What are your spiritual gifts? Pray that the Holy Spirit will reveal them to you, and if you want to grow in your spiritual gift toolbox, pray like Paul instructs in 1 Corinthians 12:31, *"Now eagerly desire the greater gifts."* Want a little help? Check out https://spiritualgiftstest.com/spiritual-gifts/[12].⇦

***

Time for A Call to Action. Write down your spiritual gifts and pray that the Holy Spirit will show you how to use them to serve others. Then find an opportunity to serve and watch God move. What I'll bet you will find is when you serve, your love meter will soar, and you'll have a heart full of gratitude.

I have one more special request: please write me at adaughtersjourney.net and share *your* serving story with me.

---

[12] https://spiritualgiftstest.com/spiritual-gifts/

Love you, Beautiful!

Till our next letter

Eve

Things to Remember:

_____

_____

_____

_____

_____

_____

_____

_____

_____

_____

_____

_____

_____

_____

_____

Chapter 10
Find Your Balance (Freedom)

*It is for freedom that Christ has set us free. Stand firm, then, and do
not let yourselves be burdened again by a yoke of slavery.*
Galatians 5:1

Hello Beautiful!

Oh happy day, it's Friday! A favorite day of the week for

students everywhere, this beloved day promises a weekend of rest,

fun, and with any luck, no homework. A particularly favorite day for

you as freedom gives you energy on the proverbial ride home from

school.

So, tell me about your day - your week. Has it been

stressful? Tell me about the blessings you found along the way; I

love to hear about God's little surprises. I know school has been a

challenge and has left you feeling defeated on occasion, but I hope

you're finding encouragement and stress relief from my previous

letters. More importantly, I hope you're seeking peace from our

Heavenly Father in the challenging and stressful moments. Just pretend Jesus and I are sitting right there with you, listening to you talk about your day and encouraging you with the words: "Stay strong. You've got this beautiful, we believe in you!" **((HUGS))**

Remember my letter when I shared the story of Elijah? We are not designed to live in a perpetual state of stress. In fact, in Luke 2 we read about a large group of angels praising God after the birth of our *Messiah* (our Savior) singing, *"Glory to God in the highest heaven, and on earth peace to those on whom his favor rests"* (Luke 2:14). In John 14:27, Jesus says to His disciples, *"Peace I leave with you, my peace I give to you, I do not give as the world gives, do not let your heart be troubled, do not be afraid."* As your Savior, Jesus came to bring you grace, He came to bring you love and He came to give you His peace.

I know, it's easy for me to say the words, "Don't worry, be happy," and I realize it's a challenge to live them, so in this letter I'd like to share some practical ways that help me to find balance, and hopefully will help you as well.

***

Stop and smell the flowers

On a beautiful summer day as I was taking a walk during lunch, the sky was blue and flowers were blooming. Singing along to a worship song, I looked up and witnessed a gift I will never forget as a perfectly formed flock of geese flew overhead. You may not consider this to be anything worth writing home about, but this moment actually changed my life. You see, we can spend a lifetime looking for the destination, but in that moment I realized that *the journey leads us to our destination.*

The sky appeared more blue, the flowers more vibrant, my breath seemed to slow, and my pupils dilated. I felt as if the Creator of the Universe had knelt down and met me where I was while providing a flyover for my enjoyment. I was awed by His glory!

Our old friend David knew what it was like to stop and smell the flowers. In Psalm 19:1-4a he writes, *"The heavens declare the glory of God; the skies proclaim the work of his hands. Day after day they pour forth speech; night after night they reveal knowledge.*

They have no speech they use no words: no sound heard from them.

Yet their voice goes out into all the earth, their words to the ends of

the world." David knew a secret we may have yet to realize, **God's**

glory speaks from the mouth of all creation, into the hearts of

those who have opened the door to His goodness. In the midst of

His glory, we learn to, *"Be still and know that He is God"* (Psalm

46:10). When we open our hearts to Him and learn to stop and

enjoy His creation, our lives become sweeter, and peace becomes

reality.

⇨**Reflection Time:** How often do you look up? How often

do you really take in the blessings that your Father has for

you? I promise you there is a surprise around every corner,

so I challenge you to be on the lookout and begin to journal

all the little blessings He sends you.⇦

***

It *really* is the little things.

As I sit in front of a lovely fire alongside my husband who is enjoying a lively football game, I write this letter to you. It's a quiet afternoon, and our beautiful basset fur-babies, Max and Belle, are curled up at our feet. The temptation to escape into the world of social media is strong. I find myself escaping way too often into the distraction provided by a scrolling newsfeed, but I realize how many little things I miss when I do so. The little conversations, the little ideas and the little moments of peace provide for rich relationships, innovation and restoration, but distractions can keep us from noticing them. **Distractions can rob us of the rich beauty of today as we find ourselves immersed in yesterday or tomorrow.**

⇨**Reflection Time:** How much time do you spend allowing distractions to keep you from living in the moment? It's okay; this is a struggle we all face. Seek ways to distance yourself from the distraction by enjoying little things in the moment, and joy will ultimately follow. Going to take a break now and cuddle with my fur-babies.⇦

***

Find the Beauty in the Wait

I remember our first microwave and the joy of being able to cook a meal in minutes with little effort. It would take several years for me to realize, however, what we would lose in the name of convenience. Pre-packaged would replace homemade, fast replaced flavorful, and instant replaced slow-cook. Please understand, I'm not bashing one of the greatest inventions of the 20th century, but it does shed light on our desire to live an instant life. Consider the question: *"Does anything good in life happen in an instant?"*

Why wait, when we have everything at our fingertips?

Why indeed? It's time to upset the apple cart again.

The greatest things on earth cannot be microwaved - love, patience, joy, hope, wisdom, strength, and even life, all take time.

> The greatest things on earth cannot be microwaved.

When you look back on your life, what will you see? Instant moments taped to one another by schedules and selfies, or will timeless moments spent enjoying those around you be interwoven into this beautiful tapestry called life? Learning to find beauty in the wait allows you to enjoy moments of love, patience, joy, hope, wisdom and strength as they weave together memories you carry for all of your life.

⇨**Reflection Time:** How do we find beauty in the wait? Put the phone down, turn the TV off, look the people around you in the eye and smile. Dance in the kitchen, laugh often and don't take yourself so seriously. And-- one of my faves-- journal, write like nobody will ever read it and share like everyone will. Learn to color, paint, draw, and play the piano or guitar. Sing around a campfire, talk through the wee hours of the morning, build a sandcastle or snowman. Write a book. **You can't find an app for timeless moments such as these.**⇦

***

Nurture your relationships.

Transitioning from a microwave to a slow-cooker can be difficult but so rewarding. Not only do you get to choose the ingredients, but you have the opportunity to engage in the blending of flavors that bring joy to the palette. Whereas a microwave allows you to make many meals quickly, a slow-cooker only allows for one meal and requires time to marinate.

Relationships, too, require time and nurturing to bring joy. When nurtured, family and friend relationships enrich your heart as you choose to love. Remember the letter I wrote about who loves you? When we nurture the relationships around us, we are sharing the love our Father so freely gives!

⇨**Reflection Time:** Beautiful, is there a relationship you have been trying to micro-cook? *Jehovah-Jireh* (God our Provider) is in the healing business. Ask Jesus to heal the broken bonds and allow forgiveness to mend the pain. God's love will serve to marinate your heart when you nurture the relationships He has placed in your path.⇦

***

Don't avoid Conflict.

Beautiful, I'm going to upset your apple cart yet again, but don't give up on me just yet. I too *do not* like conflict. When faced with this little bugger, I want to run far away. I have always believed conflict to be a waste of time. Why argue anyway? I mean, doesn't God say

> Don't avoid conflict

"Where there is strife, there is pride" (Proverbs 13:10)? Yes, this is true, but to read the first half of this scripture is to read the second half: *"but wisdom is found in those who take advice."* Ouch! To take advice means we have must be engaged and listen.

But I don't wanna! (Jumping up and down).

Just like trials and challenges are inevitable, so is conflict, and if you've been reading the book of Proverbs, you will notice quite a few references to my NOT favorite thing. Consider this instruction:

> *"Hatred stirs up conflict, but love covers all wrongs"* (Proverbs 10:12).
>
> *"A hot-tempered person stirs up conflict, but the one who is patient calms a quarrel"* (Proverbs 15:18).
>
> *"The greedy stir up conflict, but those who trust in the Lord will prosper"* (Proverbs 28:25).

Do you see the common attribute of these verses? Each has two parts, an action and a reaction. The reactions are where I believe we need to soak for a moment. When we learn to apply the fruits of the spirit to the action, we allow the peace of the Holy Spirit to fill our circumstance. Can you relate to either of these challenges?

Love – Someone gossips over a circumstance in your life. You can reciprocate through hate OR you can choose to love them and diffuse the situation.

Patience – A friend is angry at you. You could return the

anger OR listen patiently to their concerns. Seeking forgiveness goes a long way to melt a cold heart.

Trust – A co-worker wants your job and complains incessantly about your performance. You could complain OR you could trust in God and pray for Him to work through you and bless the work of your hands.

⇨**Reflection Time:** Are you afraid of conflict? Do you allow drama, strife, anger and hatred to boil up inside? When faced with conflict, engage in the "Tender Ten." Take ten seconds to calm your heart, say a quiet prayer for peace and ask God to help you listen while applying love and patience. Love will go much farther than having the last word. And God will build resilience within when you follow His plan for conflict resolution.⇦

***

Fruit of the Spirit

When I was a little girl, I loved the seesaw. Well that's until someone jumped on the other side and jerked me up and down.

Life can be like that, can't it?

In several of our letters we've addressed some of the things that can jerk our life out of balance. But the honest truth is that a seesaw can be quite fun when two people alternate in harmony.

Remember the fruits of the spirit that I shared in God's great love story? When Jesus left us his peace, He sent us a Helper in the Holy Spirit. We are children of God called to be free, to love Him and to love our neighbor. Our Helper helps us to do these things using the spiritual gifts found in the toolbox He has given us. When we allow the Holy Spirit to work in our life, He blesses us with his fruit including *"love, joy, peace, forbearance (patience), kindness, goodness, faithfulness, gentleness and self-control"* (Galatians 5:22-23a). When we work in harmony with our Helper, we experience great joy as He *helps* us navigate the ups and downs in life, guiding us into balance all while blessing us with His fruit.

⇨**Reflection Time:** A relationship with Jesus is greater than any relationship you will ever have. Dear one, I pray that in all of my letters, you see the common theme

that God loves you so much. Jesus came to give you life to

the full (John 10:10b). The full life He promises includes the

promised Helper in the Holy Spirit. After we ask Jesus into

our life, the Holy Spirit goes to work awakening our spiritual

gifts, applying His fruits to our life, all the while pouring

God's love and grace into our hearts. All of these gifts draw

us closer to the One who created us. He is the One who died

for us, the One who takes our sin and gives us grace and the

One who heals our heart and gives us peace. He's the One

who works to make us holy and righteous in Christ as He

aligns us to His heart.

Do you know Jesus? True balance and freedom can

only be found in Him! If you don't know His peace, love, and

grace, I would like to make you a promise-- **you can**! I would

love to introduce you to Him. Check out page 192. I'm

praying for you Beautiful!⇦

***

Focus on your Priorities.

Where is your focus, Beautiful? With the seesaw, if the plank isn't centered perfectly and you aren't focused on your partner, harmony becomes quite the challenge. Balance in life depends on focus as well. Does this sound counter-intuitive to what society teaches? I know, you've been led to believe that multitasking is a skill, but perhaps it isn't quite the skill we once thought? Go ahead and do a search on Google[13]. You'll find that multitasking creates brain drain and potentially damages long-term brain health.

***

But can we change our focus?

Archery is so cool, but takes great focus. You may try to target multiple arrows at the bullseye, but only one arrow focused

---

[13] https://www.google.com/

on the center has a chance of meeting the target. In your life, a lot of good opportunities will come your way, but only a few God-opportunities. Beautiful, it is critical that you know the difference.

Remember the analogy of chocolate and strawberry ice cream? It's important also to remember the world will attempt to provide 50 more flavors as alternatives, but you must still know the difference between just a good option and the option that God provides.

"Seek first his kingdom and his righteousness and all these things will be added to you as well" (Matthew 6:33).

⇨**Reflection Time:** What are you focused on, Beautiful? How do you spend your precious time? Are you finishing well or doing the bare minimum so you can bounce to the next thing? Are you living or just surviving? It doesn't matter how busy you are, if your soul is not filled and refilled, then an emptiness will gnaw at you. Beautiful, when you focus on God first as the target and keep Him in your sight, everything else will fall into place.⇦

***

Learn to Rest.

I cannot stress to you enough how important learning to rest will become. Don't misunderstand, I don't mean sleeping until noon on the weekends. We can attempt to find peace on our own by sleeping away our problems or hiding from them. We can allow fear, anxiety, stress and worry to wrap us up into a cocoon of exhaustion. But this little getaway is only temporary and peace will elude you in the long run.

We can only find true peace in the freedom of Christ. When we learn to rest in Him, He takes our burdens and gives us peace.

"Come to me, all you who are weary and burdened, and I will

give you rest" (Matthew 11:28).

Even for daughters of the Living God, rest can be camouflaged under our "To-Do" list; we can do all the right things, but still miss the point of a relationship with Christ. He wants us to rest in Him. He doesn't expect us to come to Him perfect, ***He wants*** *to meet us where we are*. He doesn't ask us to strive to do everything; instead, *He wants to help us*. He doesn't want to be an appointment in our schedule, but *He wants to draw near to us.* If we can't micro-cook our earthly relationships, what makes us think we can do it in our relationship with our Heavenly Father? No Beautiful, we can't. He wants us to live in Him as daughters of the King. To do this we have to look to Him first for all things: our identity, our relationships, our purpose, our challenges, our blessings, and our serving opportunities. And here's the thing, **when we rest in Him and make Him our priority, we free Him up to bless everything that comes after.**

***

What does a relationship with Christ look like?

Glad you asked!

First, seek a relationship with Him. Check out page 192 if you would like to know how.

Find a Bible-based church that will point you to Jesus and

encourage you to grow in your faith.

Follow Jesus in the act of baptism. An outward reflection of your inward heart, baptism represents Jesus dying and resurrecting for our sins. Baptism allows us to share with the world that we also have died to our sins and are resurrected in Him.

Surround yourself with others who are also on a path to know Him. Allow those who know Jesus to encourage you. I'm not asking for you to turn away from friendships with those who are not believers, but remember that God will provide others to encourage you. He will also send you to encourage others. This, Beautiful, is the beauty of the church.

Pray and read His word. Remember Proverbs 4:20-22 tells us to *listen carefully to His words and let them penetrate deep into our hearts.* We do this by reading His love letter to us, prayerfully studying and seeking Him through His Word.

Finally, serve Him. Jesus calls us to love Him and to love others, and there's no greater way to do that than by serving. *What does serving look like?* Well, I shared with you some great stories from some of my friends, but know that service comes in all shapes and sizes. Remember your spiritual gifts? Start there and allow God to grow the spirit of service in your heart.

Please know, dear one, that when you have a relationship with Jesus, life will not be perfect. You will continue to face challenges and maybe even depression and fear. The difference is that when we seek Him first, we allow *El Shaddai, the* Almighty God, the *great I AM,* to go to work on these things on our behalf. We learn to rest in Him while He fights for us. This is where we find true freedom.

Greater than the freedom found on a Friday ride home, His freedom grants eternal life with Him by your side.

⇨**Reflection Time:** Beautiful, what is keeping you from resting? Are you worried, are you stressed? Are you living in yesterday or tomorrow, trying to make everything work on your own? Are you not taking time with your Heavenly Father?

May I issue this challenge? Seek to live in the present

moment, remembering He is with you always and wants to give you rest. ⇐

* * *

A Call to Action: Set a time of day when you can find a quiet place, close your eyes for a few moments and breathe deeply, in and out. Visualize Jesus sitting with you. I like to whisper His name in my breath **Yah** (in) **Weh** (out) *(pronounced Yah-Weh)*. Thank Him for His presence and pray that He will give you wisdom. Then open your eyes and open His Word. Continue to get to know Him better through scripture. Afterward, just sit and talk with your Abba Father as He leads you beside quiet waters and restores your soul. And don't forget to journal all the wonderful things the Holy Spirit breathes into you!

Rest well, Beautiful!

Love you

Eve

Things to Remember:

_____

_____

_____

_____

_____

_____

_____

_____

_____

_____

_____

_____

_____

Chapter 11
You Can (and Will) Change the World

For we are God's masterpiece. He has created us anew in Christ Jesus, so we can do the good things he planned for us long ago. Ephesians 2:10 NLT

Hello Beautiful!

We've reached the end of our journey together, and I want you to know I'm so thankful for all we've shared. I know God has you on an amazing journey, and I'm so thankful that He has allowed me to play even a small part. While you will place these letters in a drawer, I pray you've written many reminders in your journal that will serve you well in the future, reminders that you can grasp in those moments of uncertainty.

Today, I have one last thing to share with you in this, my final letter.

How many times have you heard the question, "What do

you want to do when you grow up?" Oh my, here comes the anxiety; the pressure created by that one question reminds me of Granny's pressure cooker on a Sunday afternoon.

Allow me to ease the pressure a bit with a different question: **If you could do one small thing to change the world TODAY, what would it be?**

Think of every day as the connection of many small moments, and within each moment, a choice.

We learned in a previous letter how to choose our reaction within the moment, but lets up the ante a bit and discuss being proactive by asking ourselves, *"Is there something I can do **today** that can change the world?"*

You may be asking, ***"But I'm young, what can I do?"***

Let me challenge you with this: Where your passion meets the world's need, there you will find your purpose. Allow me to elaborate.

One Act of Random Kindness at a Time

Have you seen the movie, *Pay It Forward?* If you haven't, I highly suggest you watch.

Trevor Mckinney goes on a journey of exploration as part of a social studies project. The assignment is to think of something to change the world and put it into action. He wants to prove that essentially all people have good within, so he sets out to change the notion of "returning the favor" to "**pay it forward.**" The rules of the project are simple: You must do something nice for three new people and ask them to "pay it forward." I won't spoil the movie for you, but he went a long way to change the world for himself, his mom, his teacher and complete strangers as well!

Doing something nice doesn't have to be complicated. A smile in the grocery store, doing chores for family without being asked, getting coffee for a stranger or buying lunch for the person behind you. Perhaps we could give gloves to the Salvation Army bell ringer or donate for a summer camp or mission trip. Consider free gifts such as opening the door for someone or praying for someone, even for your parents. Paying it forward becomes more than a transactional way of serving, but a way of life. Paying it forward paves the way for joy to enter your journey as much as it touches those you serve!

I have some friends who have some awesome God stories to share regarding ways kindness changed their world.

***

Read Trisha's story on giving:

> "*T*he first time my daughter went to Guatemala, we were amazed to see the support money come in before she even sent out all of the support letters!"

Debbie has a story to share on prayer:

> "*I* was at the church one Monday evening helping out for an event. That night included a prayer time where people could come to be prayed over by a Pastor. I noticed a lady in the lobby, and she looked lost. I asked if I could help her, and she said she was there for prayer, so I took her where she needed to go, but the Pastor was with someone else. She looked like she was going to cry. I asked her if I could pray for her. She told me she and her husband did not have jobs, and she was afraid of the future. I prayed for her and then went on with my evening working at another event. A few months later she ran over to me and said I was her angel and she would never forget me. She called me by my name, hugging me. (I honestly had no clue who she was. Our time together was so brief).
> She said after our prayer, both she and her husband found

jobs, and she started going to our church, and she said it was my prayer that got her through it. I felt so small in God's world; I did not recognize that I had become part of her blessing. I cry when I think about it because God used me to pray for and with her in a moment that seemed like no big deal for me. Prayer is now a part of me."

There is a story I would like to share:

In an earlier letter I mentioned that I've experienced some pretty difficult circumstances. I can't sugarcoat this, so I'll come right out with it. In 2003 I was diagnosed with a rare disease. My body creates tumors that like to wrap around my carotid artery and vagus nerves; they're like extra brain mass just looking for a place to live. Thankfully, they are benign but can grow quickly; therefore, I had to make a quick decision for surgery. I wasn't a stranger to surgery, but this one was different, and I have to admit the fear I experienced as I waited was excruciating.

I felt as if my days were numbered. A young mom with two young boys, I cried out to God to give me a chance, to allow me to watch them grow up. Today I can thankfully share that God answered my prayer, and I'm still here. But something happened I will never forget: God knelt down and touched me through the hearts of a handful of people who didn't know me and probably weren't even aware of the life they changed. On the night before I had to go to the hospital, we opened the door to these total strangers who asked if they could pray for us. Yes, you read it right; they wanted to pray for us—the night before my surgery. I've never experienced this on my doorstep in my life, not before, not since. But I know without a doubt that God used these beautiful people to fill my heart with peace. I cannot tell you the impact this had on my faith journey.

Oh Beautiful, I do hope you see the love God weaves through each of us when we choose kindness. It is a choice, but one He uses over and over to change the hearts and lives of millions on a journey that ultimately leads to Him. Young Trevor had no idea the impact he would have by showing kindness to three people. Trisha was delighted to know God was using others to pour into her daughter's life. Debbie was so excited to be written into God's story for a complete stranger, and I was honored and blessed to have a Father who met me where I was on my journey and brought me comfort through the prayers of a handful of strangers standing in the gap for me. Just as Isaiah 55 promises, everything God sends out will return to Him, so His Word does not return void and neither does His love.

And you get to be part of His great story too!!!

***

Dreams, Passions and Goals

Speaking of the journey, do you still have the list of dreams and goals we discussed? Pull it out and say these words, *"Life is not about the destination, it's about the journey."* Now repeat it. If you must, write it down. We all have dreams and goals in life, and the honest truth is some of them will come to fruition and perhaps others won't, but I just love what Cinderella said:

"When you can dream, then you can start. A dream is a wish you make with your heart." [14]

I wonder if Cinderella was inspired by the promise, *"Take delight in the Lord, and he will give you the **desires of your heart**?"* Psalm 37:4 gives us a glimpse into the heart of our Father. A Father who delights in granting us the desires of our heart. Why is this? First, I think that it should be said that God is not a vending machine looking to dole out blessings when asked. But truly, when we delight in God, we are obeying Him, we are aligning with His will, and in this God reaches down to grant us what He knows we truly desire as He shares with us the true definition of unconditional love.

---

[14] http://www.metrolyrics.com/a-dream-is-a-wish-your-heart-makes-lyrics-drew-k.html

Unconditional love drove God the Son to leave the beauty and comfort of heaven to be born in a manger, and it filled Him as He taught twelve disciples the love of the Father, asking them to share it with the world. Unconditional love led Him to a lowly cross to bear the sins of every man and woman, so they could spend eternity with Him. That same love flows through God the Holy Spirit as He pours into every son and daughter and points them to the Father.

Unconditional love flowed from the heart of God the Father into a heart-broken mom afraid of losing her life and leaving young children behind.

Guess what? That same unconditional love is for you too. When you turn to Jesus and follow Him, you will see through the eyes of the One who loved you first, and in this love you will want to be obedient, and you will desire to know Him more. Love is so much more than chasing a passion. Passions fade and die, but the One who knows the count of every hair on your head also planted dreams within your heart. And He wants you to know Him too.

So, knowing that you have an empowering Heavenly Father who wants to give you the desires of your heart, I ask you again: **If you could do one thing to change the world today, what would it be?** Allow yourself to dream big because you serve a God who stands outside of space and time, who placed the stars in the sky and knows them all by name. The impossible is powerless against the One who can do the impossible and He can certainly help you carry out the dreams of your heart!

***

Thinking outside the Box

Check out this amazing but true story.

In 1809, Louis Braille was born in Coupvray, France. When he was only three years old, an eye injury left him blind. While studying at the Royal Institute for Blind Youth in Paris, Louis invented a system of reading and writing for the blind involving raised dots, today you know this as the Braille system. Studies have shown that congenitally legally blind adults who learned to read using Braille have higher employment rates and educational levels, are more financially self-sufficient, and spend more time reading than did those who learned to read using print.[15]

Braille's courage in adversity is a reminder that through the challenges we face in our journey, we have deep within us the strength to persevere and realize the dreams and goals that have found their way into our hearts.

Wow, what a story! And guess what? You have one too. Allow me to encourage you with a challenge given by Dr. John Edmund Haggai:

"Dare to attempt something so great for God that it is doomed to fail unless God is in it."

---

[15] https://www.mnn.com/lifestyle/responsible-living/photos/8-amazing-kids-who-have-changed-the-world/louis-braille#top-desktop

Sound like a big ask?

Before you say, *"that's not for me,"* let's read the stories of

ordinary people in God's Word

who, like Braille, did

extraordinary things for God!

> Dare to attempt something SO GREAT for God that it is doomed to fail unless God is in it.

- **Noah**, an ordinary man who found grace in God's sight amid a godless generation, was used to build the ark.
- **Abraham**, a friend of God, left the comforts of his home to become the father of God's chosen people.
- **Joseph**, an ordinary brother, and eventual slave was used to feed his people during famine.
- **Moses**, adopted son and eventual murderer, was used to lead his people out of slavery in Egypt.
- **Joshua**, an ordinary man with great faith, led God's people to defeat Jericho.
- **Rahab**, a prostitute, believed God and saved Joshua's spies.
- **Esther**, an ordinary Jewish girl, was used by God to turn the head of the Persian King Xerxes and save her people from extermination.
- Remember **Gideon**? While he was threshing wheat, God called this unsuspecting Mighty Warrior to lead an army of 300 farmers and shepherds to defeat 135,000 Midianites.
- Then we have our friend **David**, a lowly shepherd boy, who became a great king.
- God used **Nehemiah**, an ordinary Jewish cupbearer to the King of Persia, to lead his people to build a wall.
- **Jonah**, a rebel, was used to save a city.
- Young **Mary**, after being told she would carry the Savior of the world in her womb, courageously answered, "I am the

Lord's servant, may your word to me be fulfilled."
- **Paul**, one of the greatest persecutors of the early Christian Church, became one of the greatest missionaries of his time.

Beautiful don't miss this. Take a moment and soak in the truth of their life examples:

1- These were ordinary people.

2- They didn't know what tomorrow would bring.

3- They trusted anyway.

4- Many of them didn't get to see God's promise to them come to fruition in their lifetime.

5- Yet, they **lived on purpose** and embraced the big picture God had for them.

God has such an amazing plan. Can you imagine, just like the obedient, beautiful souls above, you get to be part of his great story! **Every unique quality He created within you is a complement to the beauty of His creation.** As a painting can't exist without the colors and textures that make up its beauty, so our Father's living creation is waiting for you to breathe *your* ideas, *your* love and _**your**_ creativity into each stroke of His brush. Be encouraged by the words of Walt Emerson,

> "**W**hat lies behind us and what lies before us are tiny matters compared to what lies within us."

So Beautiful, what are your dreams and goals? What one small step can you take today to bring one dream to fruition? It could be saying a prayer, making a phone call or even writing a list. It could be filling out that college application, going on a mission trip or walking the Appalachian Trail. It could be building the next avant-garde invention, discovering the cure for cancer or designing the next brilliant pollution reducer. It could be serving your loved ones, finding the light in others or pouring into the next generation. The point is to **do** instead of **wish.** Consider where you are today and where you want to go; then allow your journey to take you there. Put one foot in front of the other, trusting that _the Great I Am,_ the One who knows all the days ordained for you, will establish your steps and prepare you for the amazing journey to come.

✳✳✳

My final **call to action** is for you is to read from Hebrews 11 the amazing stories of ordinary people God used to do the extraordinary. And if you would like some extra credit, you can read up on some amazing women God used such as:

- Sarah (Genesis 15, Hebrews 11:11),
- Miriam (Exodus 2, 15),
- Hannah (1 Samuel 1-2),
- Jehosheba (2 Kings 11:2),
- Deborah (Judges 4:1-10),
- Ruth (Book of Ruth),
- Esther (Book of Esther),
- Mary (Luke 1:26-56),
- Elizabeth (Luke 1:41),
- Mary Magdalene
- Mary of Bethany (John 12:1-8),
- The Samaritan Woman (John 4:1-42),
- Priscilla (Acts 18:26)
- Lydia (Acts 16:11-40)
- Lois and Eunice (2 Timothy 1:3-5)

Allow their stories of obedience, courage and strength given by our empowering Father in Heaven, to inspire you to step into His plan for you.

Okay, no excuses, 1 Timothy 4:12 encourages, *"Don't let anyone look down on you because you are young, but set an example for the believers in speech, in life, in love, in faith and in* purity."

You've got this, Beautiful! I believe in you!

Eve

Things to Remember:

_____

_____

_____

_____

_____

_____

_____

_____

_____

_____

_____

_____

_____

_____

_____

FINAL THOUGHTS

Well Beautiful, our time together is complete. Thank you for allowing me this moment to share God's heart with you. I wish I could walk alongside you and hear everything God has done and is doing in your life. I truly believe He will move in your life just as He has done for so many people before you.

As we close our time today, I want to leave you these reminders:

1. Know that you are loved, regardless of what has happened in your life to lead you into believing otherwise. Your Heavenly Father loves you more than anyone else ever could or will. Through a relationship with Him, you will realize that Love is so much more than a four letter word, but is in fact a gift from the One who is Love and values you unconditionally.

2. God left us with His Word, the Bible, the greatest love story ever told. From cover to cover, He shares with us a story of love and redemption as He reveals His Son and the beautiful

sacrifice that redeems us and aligns our story with His. I encourage you to read it daily. Dig into God's Word and allow Him to show you His heart and the beauty He has for you as His daughter.

3. You are beautiful! I will never stop telling you that! God declared you fearfully and wonderfully made in His image, created through Christ. When the Father looks on you, He sees His Son along with all of the unique intricacies that He designed within you. Never forget this truth!

4. God defined you Beautiful, He knows you. He knows when you sit and when you rise; He knows your thoughts and is familiar with all your ways. When you accept Him into your life, His Spirit is with you, always guiding you, holding you fast. God created your inmost being, and He knit you together in your mother's womb. Praise Him, for you are fearfully and wonderfully made! When you were made in the secret place, you were woven together by His hand as He saw your unformed body and ordained each day for you

in His book before even one of them came to be. Allow our Creator to search you, to know your heart, to test you and know your anxious thoughts, and lead you in the way everlasting (Psalm 139 paraphrased). Remember to guard your heart, Beautiful, and don't allow others to try to re-define what He has already defined.

5. Dear one, you have a purpose, yes you! God has a purpose uniquely designed for you, and if I know nothing else about you, I know this, His purpose will prevail. I want you to remember these words: "Every day is a page in the story of {Insert your name here.} Every day draws you closer to Him as He weaves your chapter into His and draws you near. Nothing happens by accident, but by design, to develop you into the amazing woman He has called you to be."

6. Beautiful, you will face trials, but please remember you have a Helper to walk with you through them. Some days you will walk side by side, and others He will carry you. I am praying for you as you face the trials of anxiety, fear, stress and

worry, praying that you will seek Him and find His strength interwoven in peace. You can do this; I believe in you!

7. In addition to trials, I want to encourage you as you face dark seasons in your life. Whether this encouragement is for you or a friend, don't be afraid to turn on the light in the dark. Remember, darkness is only the absence of light, and when the light comes on the darkness has to flee. Your Father loves you so very much and wants to take your hand and draw you to His light. Draw near to Him and to those He places in your life to give you hope.

8. Along with trials and dark seasons in life, you will face challenges, it's inevitable. Just never forget that a challenge is nothing more than a hill to climb. So lace up those tennies, place one foot in front of the other and climb that hill! Trust Him, depend on Him, guard your heart, take captive your thoughts and face your challenges with Him by your side. You've got this, and He's got you! Oh and don't forget to seek the blessings, both small and large; they are there I

promise! (More than likely, on the other side of that hill!)

9. Serving will bring you close to the heart of God. Just as Jesus shared with his disciples, *"The King will reply, 'Truly I tell you, whatever you do for one of the least of these brothers and sisters of mine, you did for me'"* (Matthew 25:40 paraphrased). Serve others, and you will serve Him. His blessings will shine down on you.

10. Seek focus in your life. Place God first, and He will set everything else into place for you. When you focus on Him, He will balance your life and give you freedom in return.

11. He will change the world through you, Beautiful. I guarantee it! Recognize the gifts that are natural to you, and step into them. Find one thing you can do today to engage His heart in your life, and watch your beautiful story unfold.

I will miss our time together! So will you do me a favor please? Connect with me at www.adaughtersjourney.net. You can email me directly, and I would love to hear your story and would be so honored to share with you the daily blessings God is laying on my heart.

And don't forget to #findthelight. I believe that we too can change the world in which we live by shining and sharing His Light for all the world to see!

I Love you, Beautiful!

Eve

Abba Father, I thank You for every woman, young and old, who has this labor of love in their hands. I pray, Lord, that they will seek You first and trust You with all their heart. I pray, Father, that they will see themselves through Your eyes and will love others through Your Heart. I pray, Almighty God, that You will grant them wisdom and discernment in their walk and that You will help them to see the light within themselves and others. Father, strengthen each of us in our challenge and help us to see the blessings you have given. I pray that You will bless the work of their hands and their hearts as they choose to serve You. Help them to find their balance and to see the strength they have in Christ to change the world. Lord, inspire their hearts to see themselves as the Mighty Warriors You have declared them to be.

And bless each one in Jesus' holy and precious name,

AMEN

Beautiful, do you know Jesus?

God's love story written over two thousand years ago gives you the opportunity to not only know your Creator but also to know the One who came to redeem and give you eternal life! And while eternity may seem far away, the truth is that a relationship with Christ begins a full life for you now. Yes, TODAY!

Jesus came to earth to live among us, teaching us how to live and love. Through His sacrifice, our debt was paid so we can know true freedom in Him. At the Cross, He took on **our** sins, **our** shame, **our** guilt, and He covered them with **His** blood, paying **our** debt and making us clean in the process. His resurrection returned Him to the right hand of the Father where He became our High Priest, and the enemy can no longer condemn us to the Father when we say yes to Him. Jesus redeemed and restored us, but, we must accept His gift of grace. Today can be the first day of the rest of your life in His perfect peace.

Will you pray with me?

"Heavenly Father, I know You love me. I admit I

have gone my own way. But today I confess my sin; I ask you

to forgive me through the sacrifice of Jesus and change my

heart. Give me the hope of eternal life as today I come home

to you. Thank You for the freedom found in you. In Jesus'

Name amen."

YAY my sister in Christ! I am so happy for you. In

this very moment I am praying that you will seek Him, trust

Him and enjoy a beautiful and rich relationship with Jesus

for all of your days!

I hope through these letters, that you take away this truth: God's

Word is filled with all we need to live a full life. The resources found

in these letters make up only a small piece of the glory that God has

to show you. Join a Bible based church and surround yourself with

others who are seeking the full life that Christ has to give.

I challenge you to write down the resources from these

letters and commit them to memory. Perhaps even go on a treasure

hunt to find additional scriptures that speak most to you and your

circumstance.

I am praying for you in this very moment that He will bless you and keep you.

Oh, and don't forget to reach out to me, I would love to hear your story. And if we don't meet on this side of eternity, well look me up at the wedding feast, I will save a seat for you.

I Love you, Beautiful!

Eve

RESOURCES

YOU ARE LOVED

"For as high as the heavens are above the earth, so great is his love for those who fear him." (Psalm 103:11)

"You have searched me, Lord, and you know me. You know when I sit and when I rise; you perceive my thoughts from afar." (Psalm 139:1)

"For you created my inmost being; you knit me together in my mother's womb. I praise you because **I AM FEARFULLY AND WONDERFULLY MADE**; your works are wonderful, I know that full well. My frame was not hidden from you when I was made in the secret place, when I was woven together in the depths of the earth. Your eyes saw my unformed body; all the days ordained for me were written in your book before one of them came to be. How precious to me are your thoughts God! How vast is the sum of them! Were I to count them, they would outnumber the grains of sand- when I awake, I am still with you." (Psalm 139:13-18)

THE GREATEST LOVE STORY

"For God so loved the world that he gave his one and only Son, that whoever believes in him shall not perish but have eternal life." (John 3:16)

"The thief comes only to steal and kill and destroy; I have come that they may have life, and have it to the full." (John 10:10)

"The fruit of the Spirit is love, joy, peace, forbearance (patience), kindness, goodness, faithfulness, gentleness and self-control. (Galatians 5:22-23a)

"My child, pay attention to what I say. Listen carefully to my words. Don't lose sight of them. Let them penetrate deep into your heart, for they bring life to those who find them and healing to their whole body." (Proverbs 4:20-22 NLT)

YOU ARE BEAUTIFUL

"You will be a crown of splendor in the Lord's hand, a royal diadem in the hand of your God." (Isaiah 62:3)

"The Lord make his face shine on you and be gracious to you." (Numbers 6:25)

"So God created mankind in his own image, in the image of God he created them; male and female he created them." (Genesis 1:27)

"God saw all that he had made, and it was very good." (Genesis 1:31a)

"Rather, it should be that of your inner self, the unfading beauty of a gentle and quiet spirit, which is of great worth in God's sight." (1 Peter 3:4)

WHO DEFINES YOU?

"See what great love the Father has lavished on us, that we should be called **children of God**! And that is what we are! The reason the world does not know us is that it did not know him." (1 John 3:1)

"He has made everything beautiful in its time. He has also set eternity in the human heart; yet no one can fathom what God has done from beginning to end." (Ecclesiastes 3:11)

"Therefore, if anyone is in Christ, the new creation has come: The old has gone, the new is here!" (2 Corinthians 5:17)

"Don't you know that you yourselves are God's temple and that God's Spirit dwells in your midst?" (1 Corinthians 3:16)

"I will be a Father to you, and you will be my sons and daughters, says the Lord Almighty." (2 Corinthians 6:18)

"But you are a chosen people, a royal priesthood, a holy nation, God's special possession, that you may declare the praises of him who called you out of darkness into his wonderful light." (1 Peter 2:9).

"Walk with the wise and become wise, for a companion of fools suffers harm." (Proverbs 13:20)

"Above all else, guard your heart, for everything you do flows from it." (Proverbs 4:23)

"Look at the birds of the air; they do not sow or reap or store away in barns, and yet your heavenly Father feeds them. Are you not much more valuable than they?" (Matthew 6:26)

YOU HAVE A PURPOSE

"For I know the plans I have for you," declares the Lord, "plans to prosper you and not to harm you, plans to give you hope and a future." (Jeremiah 29:11)

"Trust in the Lord with all your heart and lean not on your own understanding; in all your ways submit to him, and he will make your paths straight." (Proverbs 3:5-6)

"Consider it pure joy, my brothers and sisters, whenever you face trials of many kinds." (James 1:2)

"I can do all this through him who gives me strength." (Philippians 4:13)

"His divine power has given us everything we need for a godly life through our knowledge of him who called us by his glory and goodness. Through these he has given us his very great and precious promises, so that through them you may participate in the divine nature." (2 Peter 1:3-4a)

"As the rain and the snow come down from heaven, and do not return to it without watering the earth and making it bud and flourish, so that it yields seed for the sower and bread for the eater, so is my word that goes out from my mouth: It will not return to me empty, but will accomplish what I desire and achieve the purpose for which I sent it. You will go out in joy and be led forth in peace; the mountains and hills will burst into song before you, and all the trees of the field will clap their hands." (Isaiah 55:10-12)

ANXIETY, FEAR, STRESS AND WORRY

"Do not be anxious about anything, but in every situation, by prayer and petition, with thanksgiving, present your requests to God. And the peace of God, which transcends all understanding, will guard your hearts and your minds in Christ Jesus." (Philippians 4:6-7)

"Trust in the Lord with all your heart and lean not on your own understanding; in all your ways submit to him, and he will make your paths straight." (Proverbs 3:5-6)

"When hard pressed, I cried to the Lord; he brought me into a spacious place. The Lord is with me; I will not be afraid. What can mere mortals do to me? The Lord is with me; he is my helper. I look in triumph on my enemies." (Psalm 118:5-7)

"Have I not commanded you? Be strong and courageous. Do not be afraid; do not be discouraged, for the LORD your God will be with you wherever you go." (Joshua 1:9)

"Look at the birds of the air; they do not sow or reap or store away in barns, and yet your Father feeds them. Are you not much more valuable than they? Can any one of you by worrying add a single hour to your life?" (Matthew 6:26-27)

"Would not God have discovered it, since he knows the secrets of the heart?" (Psalm 44:21)

FINDING THE LIGHT IN THE DARKNESS

"In him was life, and that life was the light of all mankind. The light shines in the darkness, and the darkness has not overcome it." (John 1:4-5)

"The grace of our Lord was poured out on me abundantly, along with the faith and love that are in Christ Jesus." (1 Timothy 1:14)

"With a mighty hand and outstretched arm; His love endures forever."(Psalm 136:12)

CHALLENGES AND BLESSINGS

"Consider it pure joy, my brothers and sisters, whenever you face trials of many kinds, because you know that the testing of your faith produces perseverance. Let perseverance finish its work so that you may be mature and complete, not lacking anything." (James 1:2-4)

"I can do all this through him who gives me strength." (Philippians 4:13)

"Above all else, guard your heart, for everything you do flows from it." (Proverbs 4:23)

"Finally, brothers and sisters, whatever is true, whatever is noble, whatever is right, whatever is pure, whatever is lovely, whatever is admirable - if anything is excellent or praiseworthy - **think** about such **things**." (Philippians 4:8)

A SERVANT HEART IS A GRATEFUL HEART

"Above all, love each other deeply, because love covers over a multitude of sins. Offer hospitality to one another without grumbling. Each of you should use whatever gift you have received to serve others, as faithful stewards of God's grace in its various forms." (1 Peter 4:8-10)

"Love the Lord your God with all your heart and with all your soul and with all your mind. This is the first and greatest commandment. And the second is like it: 'Love your neighbor as yourself.'" (Matthew 22:37-39)

"There are different kinds of gifts, but the same Spirit distributes them. There are different kinds of service, but the same Lord. There are different kinds of working, but in all of them and in everyone it is the same God at work." (1 Corinthians 12:4-6)

"If one part suffers, every part suffers with it; if one part is honored, every part rejoices with it." (1 Corinthians 12:26)

"Love is patient, love is kind. It does not envy, it does not boast, it is not proud. It does not dishonor others, it is not self-seeking, it is not easily angered, it keeps no record of wrongs. Love does not delight in evil but rejoices with the truth. It always protects, always trusts, always hopes, always perseveres. Love never fails." (1 Corinthians 13:4-8a)

"Now eagerly desire the greater gifts." (1 Corinthians 12:31)

FIND YOUR BALANCE

"It is for freedom that Christ has set us free. Stand firm, then, and do not let yourselves be burdened again by a yoke of slavery." (Galatians 5:1)

"Peace I leave with you: my peace I give to you. I do not give as the world gives. Do not let your heart be troubled and, do not be afraid." (John 14:27)

"The heavens declare the glory of God; the skies proclaim the work of his hands. Day after day they pour forth speech; night after night they reveal knowledge. They have no speech, they use no words; no sound heard from them. Yet their voice goes out into all the earth, their words to the ends of the world." (Psalm 19:1-4)

"Be still, and know that I am God; I will be exalted among the nations, I will be exalted in the earth." (Psalm 46:10)

"Where there is strife, there is pride, but wisdom is found in those who take advice." (Proverbs 13:10)

"Hatred stirs up conflict, but love covers all wrongs." (Proverbs 10:12)

"A hot-tempered person stirs up conflict, but the one who is patient calms a quarrel." (Proverbs 15:18)

"The greedy stir up conflict, but those who trust in the Lord will prosper." (Proverbs 28:25) "love, joy, peace, forbearance (patience), kindness, goodness, faithfulness, gentleness and self-control." (Galatians 5:22b-23a) "The thief comes only to steal and kill and destroy; I have come that they may have life, and have it to the full." (John 10:10)

"But seek first his kingdom and his righteousness, and all these things will be given to you as well." (Matthew 6:33)

"Come to me, all you who are weary and burdened, and I will give you rest." (Matthew 11:28)

"Pay attention to what I say; turn your ear to my words. Do not let them out of your sight, keep them within your heart; for they are life to those who find them and health to one's whole body." (Proverbs 4:20-22 NIV)

YOU CAN *(WILL)* CHANGE THE WORLD

"For we are God's masterpiece. He has created us anew in Christ Jesus, so we can do the good things he planned for us long ago." (Ephesians 2:10 NLT)

"Take delight in the Lord, and he will give you the **desires of your heart**." (Psalm 37:4)

"Don't let anyone look down on you because you are young, but set an example for the believers in speech, in life, in love, in faith and in purity." (1 Timothy 4:12)

What verses would you like to add? Share them with me at:

https://youthroughthefatherseyes.com/:

_____

_____

_____

_____

_____

_____

_____

_____

_____

_____

_____

_____

_____

_____

_____

Would you like to download a printable copy of these scriptures and add more of your own?

Check out the book's website:
https://youthroughthefatherseyes.com/

Check out the playlist:
ThroughtheFather'sEyes on Spotify

Additional website resources:

https://bible.com/

https://biblegateway.com/

https://twloha.com/

https://www.gozen.com/

https://suicidepreventionlifeline.org/

http://www.brittnicole.com

I would love to hear from you!

Visit me at:
https://adaughtersjourney.net/

About The Author:

Eve Harrell and her husband, Tony serve their local church as Small Group Leaders to some amazing future leaders. In addition to serving students and their leaders, Eve encourages women of all ages to rest in the love of their Heavenly Father.

Eve and Tony are happily married and are the parents of two young men: Lee and Lance. They live in Lawrenceville, Georgia where Eve works for a local heating and air contractor.

Singing, blogging, speaking, writing, spending time in nature and watching others find freedom in Christ are some of Eve's favorite things.

Eve's passion includes encouraging the next generation to recognize the great value, purpose, and strength they have been given while finding the Father's little gifts along the way.

You can connect with her at https://adaughtersjourney.net.

Who Does God Say I Am?
(Draw a silhouette and write God's Truth inside on the page below)

Made in the USA
Columbia, SC
03 July 2023

19702772R00120